Complete
Communication Skills
Activities Kit

Complete Communication Skills Activities Kit

LeRoy Hay, Ph.D.
Richard Zboray

THE CENTER FOR APPLIED
RESEARCH IN EDUCATION
West Nyack, New York 10995

Library of Congress Cataloging-in-Publication Data

Hay, LeRoy.
   Complete communication skills activities kit / LeRoy Hay, Richard
Zboray.
     p.   cm.
   ISBN 0-87628-260-5
   1. Language arts (Secondary)—Handbooks, manuals, etc.
2. Communication—Study and teaching   (Secondary)—Handbooks,
manuals, etc. 3. Critical thinking—Study and teaching (Secondary)—
Handbooks, manuals, etc.   I. Zboray, Richard.   II. Title.
LB1631.H33   1992
428'.0071'2—dc20   91-40208
                                        CIP

ISBN 0-87628-260-5

**The Center for Applied
Research in Education**
Business Information & Publishing Division
West Nyack, NY 10995
Simon & Schuster, A Paramount Communications Company

Printed in the United States of America

ABOUT THE AUTHORS

LeRoy Hay, 1983 National Teacher of the Year, was a teacher of English and English Department Chairperson at Manchester High School in Manchester, Connecticut for twenty-three years. Currently, he is the Assistant Superintendent for the East Lyme Public Schools in East Lyme, Connecticut. In addition, Dr. Hay is an adjunct instructor for Boston College and has taught at the University of Connecticut, Manchester Community College, and Sacred Heart University in Bridgeport.

Dr. Hay's articles have appeared in *Teacher Magazine*, *Education Week*, *Educational Leadership*, and many other publications. He has served as a consultant, committee member, or reviewer for a number of educational agencies and associations, including the U.S. Department of Education, the State of Connecticut Department of Education, and the Association for Supervision and Curriculum Development. He has a special interest in Future Studies and served on the national selection committee for N.A.S.A.'s Teacher in Space Program. He has won numerous awards and honors for teaching.

Dr. Hay earned a B.A. in English Education from the State University of New York, Cortland, and both an M.A. in Theater and a Ph.D. in Curriculum and Instruction from the University of Connecticut.

Richard Zboray has worked in information industries for nineteen years and is currently Manager of Corporate Communications for a software company, Co-ordination Technology. In addition to writing about technical subjects, Mr. Zboray has prepared materials for firms including Shearson, Prudential Bache, John Hancock, and New York Life and has counseled executives on how best to present their ideas.

Mr. Zboray has published articles in *The New York Times*, *The Christian Science Monitor*, *Crosscurrents*, and regional magazines. He is the author of *Programs for Profit* (McGraw-Hill, 1983), a guide to starting and supporting businesses with a personal computer.

ABOUT THIS RESOURCE

The *Complete Communication Skills Activities Kit* provides forty-five complete lesson plans and more than ninety reproducible worksheets to help you teach students the broad range of skills they will need to work and communicate effectively in a world of vastly expanding information.

These activities can be used with any students who are already capable of writing a traditional five-paragraph essay. Designed to supplement your regular English curriculum, lessons in the *Kit* teach writing formats and specialized skills that are generally not covered in a secondary or college education, but are vital to success in the workplace. At the same time, however, they reinforce basic skills important in any academic setting.

The forty-five lessons in the *Complete Communication Skills Activities Kit* can be used in the order provided or as needed. Taught in sequence, they help you teach students the following skills:

- Listening and speaking
- Working in groups
- Brainstorming
- Understanding the audience
- Writing concisely
- Making writing look easier to read
- Writing bulleted summaries and knowing when to use them
- Organizing information in a variety of ways
- Cutting and pasting to revise
- Using body language when speaking
- Using visual aids when presenting
- Using storyboards to plan visuals
- Conceptualizing videos
- Using statistics (and understanding their potential abuse)
- Creating word pictures
- Working as part of an organization

While these lessons work extremely well in conjunction with new technology such as word processors, none is required to complete any of the activities in this resource. Lessons in conveying information visually require no artistic talent from students or special technologies from the school. Critical thinking skills are encouraged throughout, with students prompted to draw their own conclusions from examples, their work, and class discussion.

For ease of use, each classroom-tested lesson includes a short overview, student objectives, suggestions for "setting the stage," step-by-step directions for teaching the lesson, suggestions for evaluation, and/or answer keys. Motivating the students is relatively easy because they appreciate the frequent opportunity to work in groups and are generally eager to learn skills they will need in their careers.

As we head into the twenty-first century, the ability to understand and process information is becoming increasingly important. While the traditional lessons of English are irreplaceable, even our best students can benefit from knowing the strategies professionals use to manage information in the world beyond the classroom.

LeRoy Hay
Richard Zboray

CONTENTS

Section 1

Working on Basic Communication Skills

WORKING ON BASIC COMMUNICATION SKILLS

Section One focuses on speaking, listening, and teamwork skills. This overview allows you to preview the sessions and see how they fit together.

Session 1. A Classroom Demonstration of Basic Communication

Whispering a message in the ears of a chain of students is an old game, but a variation of it in this demonstration helps students analyze communication. This exercise simplifies communication to a basic "give and take." At the end of the exercise, you lead an analysis of the "give and take," and students identify what interfered with effective communication.

Session 2. Why Listening Matters

This session helps students recognize that listening is the communication skill used far more than any other. They will estimate the percentage of time they communicate in school by reading (words and images), writing, speaking, and listening. They will also estimate percentages for the workplace.

Session 3. Developing Listening Skills

Like reading, listening is a skill that can be developed. Your students will analyze a communication experience to create listening guidelines.

Session 4. Working as a Team: Brainstorming

In this session, students practice listening and speaking in a team setting. They brainstorm a team solution to a problem and then analyze the expe-

3

rience and develop guidelines for working together as a communication team. These guidelines and the brainstorming technique will be used in other sessions.

Session 5. Assuming Different Roles on a Communication Team

On communication teams, people play different roles. The class is divided into teams, and each student in each team assumes one role for about four or five minutes. Students change roles until they have had a chance to look at communication group interactions from all perspectives.

Session 6. Understanding Your Audience

So far, students have worked on skills for exchanging information informally. In this session, they prepare to work on more formal presentations (written, spoken, or visual) by focusing on the audience. Students analyze an audience to focus their message.

Session 1. A CLASSROOM DEMONSTRATION OF BASIC COMMUNICATION

At the outset, you (but not your class) should know that this exercise has the framework of an old-fashioned "bucket brigade," the kind used to extinguish fires before the advent of fire engines and hydrants.

OBJECTIVES

The students will

- Recognize that communication depends on *interaction* and *cooperation*
- Analyze what interferes with communication

SETTING THE STAGE

Tell your students they are about to learn about communicating, even though they may not think they need to learn about it. Because communicating is basic to living and everyone communicates hundreds of times every day, it is easy to overlook the skills involved. To improve these skills, however, the class will analyze how information gets into our heads and how we get it out.

For this analysis, *input* skills represent taking in information, and *output* skills represent giving information to others. Create a table in two columns on the board. The left column will show the output skills and the right column the input skills. Ask your students to identify communication skills for each column.

Output Skills	Input Skills
writing	reading
speaking	listening
imaging (creating images)	viewing (reading images)

At first, this analysis may seem too basic to bother with, but it defines the framework for all communications. This table should help the class understand that the basis of communication is interaction:

- Someone talks; others listen.
- Someone writes; others read it.
- Someone creates an illustration or video; others see it.

With this simple model, students can perform the exercise and analyze what can interfere with communication.

PROCEDURE

1. Hand out Sheet 1–1, "Whisper Brigade," and explain the exercise:
   - You will whisper a message to a student in the back of the room.
   - That student will whisper the message in the ear of the person in front of him or her and then complete the exercise sheet.
   - Each student in turn will receive and pass on the message.
   - After passing on the message, each student should write it on the exercise sheet and answer the questions.

   Note: If you have a large class, begin the message in two different locations.

2. Stress that the message is not to be repeated. A student may not understand the message, but it is not to be repeated.

3. Go to the first student and whisper:

   "Take this bucket filled to the brim with water so we can all work together to put out the fire raging in the front of the room."

4. After the last student has recorded the message and completed the exercise sheet, ask him or her to share the message with the class by writing it on the board. Then write the original message on the board.

5. Tell the class they were all volunteer firefighters, trying to put out a fire raging in the front of the room. In a bucket brigade, each person in turn takes a bucket of water and passes it to the next person. Instead of water, your students were passing along information.

6. Compare the first and last messages. Is there enough content left after the message has been passed along to put out the fire? Or was important content lost in the exchange? (If the first and last messages match, you have a truly exceptional class and should congratulate them on their keen communication skills.)

7. Use the paper trail provided by Sheet 1–1 to see how the message changed and where it broke down. Ask students in turn to read what they wrote.

8. Hand out Sheet 1–2, "Interferences in Reading and Writing," which asks students to apply their analysis of this speaking/listening interaction to writing and reading. For example, in speaking, noise distracts listeners; in writing, unnecessary information (noise) distracts readers from the main point.

DISCUSSION GUIDE

Ask your students to talk about their problems in giving and getting information. Use their experiences as captured on Sheet 1–1 in the discussion.

Ask the class whether it would have helped to know about the fire brigade framework in the beginning. That framework, or context, would have clued them into some key words (fire, bucket, water) that would have helped the message to "sink in" easier. One important interference in communication can be a missing or unclear context. Other interferences may be

- The speaker and listener must establish a common bond. The speaker may have spoken faster than the other person was prepared to listen.
- The listener didn't focus on the message.
- The listener tried to understand before hearing the message.
- Creativity interfered with accuracy; the listener added to the message.
- The listener wasn't allowed to verify his or her understanding, so the process itself interfered with communication.

Name _____   Date _____

1–1. WHISPER BRIGADE

Directions: Answer the following questions as soon as you have passed the whispered message along to the next student.

1. Write down exactly what you heard: _____

   _____

   _____

   _____

2. Put a check next to the interferences that prevented you from accurately getting the message:

   ☐ a. The speaker was imprecise, mumbling, speaking too softly, or speaking too fast.

   ☐ b. The speaker began before you were ready.

   ☐ c. You were thinking about something else when the speaker began.

   ☐ d. Once the speaker started, you began thinking because the message wasn't making sense.

   ☐ e. Noises made it difficult for you to hear or concentrate.

   ☐ f. You tried to get the flow of the message, but you missed the exact wording.

   ☐ g. You didn't know what to expect, so you were unprepared.

   ☐ h. Other _____

   _____

3. Put a check next to the interferences that hindered you in accurately giving the message:

   ☐ a. You didn't think what you heard was right, so you changed it to make it more sensible.

   ☐ b. You never got the message, but hearing it again was against the rules, so you had to guess what was said and pass it along.

   ☐ c. You didn't think the person you were speaking to was interested.

   ☐ d. You didn't want to pass along a message that made no sense.

   ☐ e. Other _____

   _____

1–2. INTERFERENCES IN READING AND WRITING

Directions: Interferences occur in writing and reading just as in speaking and listening. Select five interferences from speaking and listening, and then list each and explain how each could also apply to reading and writing.

1. Interference: _____

_____

Applies to reading/writing: _____

_____

2. Interference: _____

_____

Applies to reading/writing: _____

_____

3. Interference: _____

_____

Applies to reading/writing: _____

_____

4. Interference: _____

_____

Applies to reading/writing: _____

_____

5. Interference: _____

_____

Applies to reading/writing: _____

_____

Session 2. WHY LISTENING SKILLS MATTER

This session helps students recognize that listening is the communication skill used far more than any other.

OBJECTIVE

The students will estimate the relative use of the four basic communication skills (reading, writing, speaking, and listening) in school and in the workplace.

SETTING THE STAGE

Studies show that when people communicate, they listen 50 to 60 percent of the time, far surpassing the usage of any other communication skill. More than any other skill, listening helps us learn information. If we don't listen well—if we "hear" the wrong information—we can't help but tell others the wrong information. That's why being a good listener is critical.

Ironically, although listening is the communication skill we use most often, it is the one we work on the least. Most schools commit large amounts of time to teaching more effective reading and writing, and even speaking, but little time to improving listening skills.

Listening, however, is a skill like reading and writing that can be developed.

PROCEDURE

1. Hand out Sheet 2–1, "Estimating Communication Skill Usage." Ask students to estimate the percentage of time they use each of the four communication skills in a day at school and then the amount of time one of their parents or a relative uses each in a typical day at work. Note that this is for time spent receiving or transmitting information but does not include entertainment (such as listening to music or watching television for fun).

2. To help students visualize the differences, ask them to draw a bar on the appropriate graph to represent each estimate.

3. Hand out Sheet 2–2, "Actual Communication Skill Usage," which shows what research has found to be the average breakdown. Have your students compare and contrast their estimates with the research.

Name _____ Date _____

2–1. ESTIMATING COMMUNICATION SKILL USAGE

Directions: In the blanks below, estimate the percentage of your communication time you spend using each of the communication skills listed during a typical day at school. Then estimate the percentage used each day by a parent or relative on a typical workday. **Note:** Do not include time spent on entertainment (such as listening to music or watching television for fun).

At School:

_____ % reading (words and images)

_____ % writing

_____ % speaking

_____ % listening

100 % total

At Work:

_____ % reading (words and images)

_____ % writing

_____ % speaking

_____ % listening

100 % total

Now draw bars (one for each skill) on each graph below to represent your estimates.

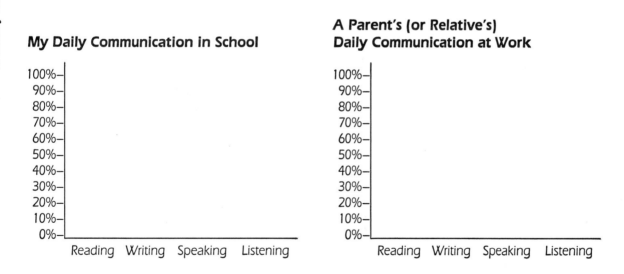

My Daily Communication in School

```
100%-
 90%-
 80%-
 70%-
 60%-
 50%-
 40%-
 30%-
 20%-
 10%-
  0%-
     Reading  Writing  Speaking  Listening
```

A Parent's (or Relative's) Daily Communication at Work

```
100%-
 90%-
 80%-
 70%-
 60%-
 50%-
 40%-
 30%-
 20%-
 10%-
  0%-
     Reading  Writing  Speaking  Listening
```

2-2. ACTUAL COMMUNICATION SKILL USAGE

Directions: The graphs below illustrate what researchers have found to be actual communication skill usage in school and at work. At the bottom of this sheet, compare and contrast your estimated usages with the research results.

Student Communication Skill Usage in School

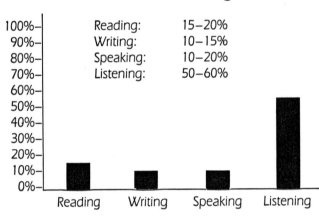

Reading:	15–20%
Writing:	10–15%
Speaking:	10–20%
Listening:	50–60%

Communication Skills in the Workplace

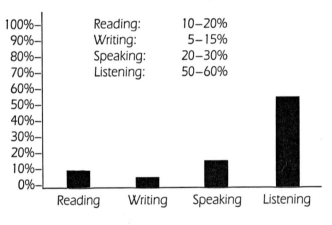

Reading:	10–20%
Writing:	5–15%
Speaking:	20–30%
Listening:	50–60%

COMPARE AND CONTRAST: _____

_____

_____

_____

_____

_____

Session 3. DEVELOPING LISTENING SKILLS

In this session, students analyze a listening experience and create listening guidelines that will serve as a reference throughout their communications work.

OBJECTIVES

The students will

- Evaluate their own listening skills
- Develop guidelines for improving listening skills

SETTING THE STAGE

At first, students may find the idea of developing listening skills hard to grasp. Is listening really a skill? Can it be developed? Point out how

- Musicians have listening skills attuned to music.
- Baseball players listen for the crack of the bat to judge how to play a fly ball.
- Doctors have highly developed listening skills to help with diagnosis.

Listening can be developed like any other skill—by working on it.

PROCEDURE

1. Ask a student (preferably one with difficulties in listening) to help you complete the script for a treasure hunt (Sheet 3–1, "Treasure Hunt Script"). This work will give the student a jump on preparing for this lesson. Or, you can complete the script yourself.
2. Inform the class that

   - The directions will be given only once, so students should listen carefully.
   - Students cannot interrupt to ask questions.
   - Students will be listening to instructions for a treasure hunt for about three minutes. They will be quizzed on details and sequences afterward.
   - It's a good idea to take accurate, detailed notes.

3. Begin reading aloud your completed Sheet 3–1. Read *slowly* and pronounce words distinctly.

4. When your presentation is complete, hand out Sheet 3–2, "Treasure Hunt Quiz."

5. Once students have completed the quiz, go over the answers with them.

6. Hand out Sheet 3–3, "Listener's Self-Evaluation." Ask students to evaluate their listening experience and develop listening guidelines.

7. As you discuss the students' experiences, hand out Sheet 3–4, "Listening Guidelines." Students should read it carefully and think about how best to apply the guidelines.

8. Finally, hand out Sheet 3–5, "Speaking Guidelines."

ANSWERS

On Sheet 3–2, "Treasure Hunt Quiz,"

- The order for A should read: 4, 5, 2, 7, 3, 1, 6.
- The answers in B will depend on your version of the script.

For possible answers to Sheet 3–3, "Listener's Self-Evaluation," see the listening guidelines on Sheet 3–4.

Name _____   Date _____

3–1. TREASURE HUNT SCRIPT

Directions: This sheet contains some fictitious directions with missing information for finding a treasure. Complete the directions by providing the missing detail asked for in the parentheses.

Since I cannot get away at this time because I am _____ (number) years old and my _____ (person) won't let me travel, I am going to trust you to retrieve the $ _____ (amount) which I buried to keep it from my _____ (relative). You and I have agreed that we will split the money, with _____ % (number) for you and _____ % (number) for me. Please note that the tape recording of these directions will self-destruct once it has played through.

On _____ (day of week) at _____ (time), take the _____ (color) bus to the corner of _____ (name) and _____ (name) streets. Get off the bus and begin to sing _____ (name of song) while you pretend to be reading a(an) _____ (name) comic book.

Be on the lookout for a woman who will be dressed in a _____ (color) raincoat and who will be carrying a(an) _____ (something found in the kitchen) in her right hand. Tell her that _____ (woman's first name) sent you to see her pet _____ (animal). She will then tell you that her pet is in _____ (name of a state) and hand you the key to a purple _____ (make of car) that is parked across the street.

Get in the car and drive straight down the road for _____ (number) blocks until you see a store that sells _____ (product). In the window will be a picture of _____ (famous politician) eating _____ (food). If the picture is of _____ (another famous politician), drive on. It is too dangerous and we'll try again in _____ (number) days. Otherwise, park the car and go into the store.

Inside the store you will see a man who will answer to the name of _____ (man's first name) and who will be wearing a hat that looks like a(an) _____

3–1. Treasure Hunt Script Continued

(animal). He will ask you if you would like to purchase a(an) _____ (article of clothing), and you should tell him you will if it is _____ (color). He will then take you out the back door of the store where you will see a boy flying a kite that is in the shape of a(an) _____ (animal).

Give the boy $ _____ (amount) for the kite. When you pull the kite in, you will find a cliché printed on it that says, "Don't count your _____ (plural object) before they're _____ (past tense verb)." Turn the kite over and you will find the picture of _____ (famous sports figure) pasted on it. Carefully pull the picture off, and you will find a map on the back of it.

Follow the map carefully, and you will end up in front of a tree that looks like _____ (famous sports figure). You'll notice that there is a hole in the tree trunk about seven feet above the ground. Reach into the hole, but be careful because I put a(an) _____ (animal) in there to protect my money and I don't know if it is still alive. Feel around in the hole and you'll find a plastic bag with the money! At least that's where I think I left it.

3-2. TREASURE HUNT QUIZ

Directions: Check the effectiveness of your listening skills by answering the following questions about the treasure hunt you just heard.

A. Can you remember the sequence of the instructions given to you? Number them from the first (#1) to the last (#7).

_____ Look for a politician's picture

_____ Buy a kite

_____ Be on the lookout for a woman

_____ Go to a special tree

_____ Drive the car

_____ Take the bus

_____ Find the map

B. Answer the following questions about recalling detail:

1. How old is the speaker? _____

2. What percentage of the money will you get? _____

3. What song should you sing? _____

4. In the store window is a picture of a politician. Who is it? _____

   What is the politician eating? _____

5. If the politician's picture isn't in the window, how many days should you wait

   before trying again? _____

6. What does the tree containing the treasure look like? _____

7. What animal is inside the tree? _____

8. How much should you give the boy for the kite? _____

9. On what day of the week should you start the hunt? _____

10. Where's the map? _____

Name _____ Date _____

3–3. LISTENER'S SELF-EVALUATION

Directions: Think back to the listening exercise you have just completed. Analyze your experience by answering the following questions:

1. What helped you to be an effective listener? List what helps a person to be a good listener.

   a. _____

   b. _____

   c. _____

   d. _____

   e. _____

2. What can you do to become an even better listener than you are right now? Try to think of a situation where you (or someone else) were not able to listen effectively. Identify what you might have done to be a better listener. Write your suggestions below.

   TO BE A BETTER LISTENER, YOU SHOULD

   a. _____

   b. _____

   c. _____

   d. _____

3. Complete this next section during the classroom discussion. List additional suggestions for becoming a better listener that you hear in the discussion:

   a. _____

   b. _____

   c. _____

3–4. LISTENING GUIDELINES

1. Treat the speaker courteously. Concentrate on what the speaker is saying, being careful not to make comments or make faces at the speaker. This could distract the speaker and interfere with other listeners.

2. Listen with pencil in hand, taking detailed notes but also listening to the general flow. Good notes about ideas and important details are essential to good listening. They also help you focus your mind on what is being said.

3. Try to identify the organizational pattern being used (such as chronological, alphabetical, by priority) so you can anticipate what might be said next.

4. If you don't understand a subject, try not to think too much about it while listening. Take exact, detailed notes and think about the talk later during a review.

5. If the rules allow, don't be afraid to ask a question about a word or term you didn't understand. Chances are that if you didn't understand, others didn't either—the speaker was not communicating well.

6. If the rules allow, interrupt (politely) to verify your understanding. An interruption early that clarifies a misunderstanding makes for more efficient communication later.

7. Try to separate important from unimportant information by using cues in the beginning of a presentation.

8. Focus on listening. Don't let your mind wander.

9. Ignore extraneous noises.

10. Remember to take notes on *the sequence* of ideas presented.

11. Distinguish between fact and opinion in what you hear. Identify the motivation and the bias of the speaker.

12. Note transition words and phrases to help you follow the speaker's logic (examples include *next, then, because of this, as a result*).

3–5. SPEAKING GUIDELINES

When speaking in a large or small group situation, remember:

1. Your first responsibility is to get your ideas across. You should not be concerned with being eloquent, just with doing what works.

2. Whenever possible, plan in advance what you are going to say. At least have a general idea of the points you want to make before you begin. Don't keep the listeners waiting, or their minds will begin to wander.

3. Do not begin speaking until the listeners are paying attention.

4. Talk about the subject at hand; do not wander off the subject. Avoid presenting information that has nothing to do with your subject.

5. Don't overwhelm your listeners with details. Begin with a general statement that will give your listeners a perspective on your thinking.

6. Use verbal guideposts such as *first*, *next*, and so on to help the listeners follow your presentation. Signal when you are about to end with a guidepost such as *finally*.

7. Speak clearly and distinctly, making sure your voice is loud enough for *all* listeners to hear. Remember, your normal speaking voice may not be loud enough when you speak to a group.

8. Let your listeners' ears adjust to the rhythm of your speech. To allow for this adjustment, do not present vital information in your first statement or two.

9. Concentrate on what you are saying. Do not let your mind wander or be distracted.

10. Use inflections in your voice and convey emotion whenever possible. Avoid speaking in a monotone. If you don't sound interested in what you are saying, don't expect your listeners to be interested.

11. Do not try to speak when someone else is speaking. The listeners will not know where to direct their attention.

12. Treat your listeners courteously. If you shout at them or insult them, they may stop listening because they are hurt or angry.

Session 4. WORKING AS A TEAM: BRAINSTORMING

The second most important communication skill is speaking. In this activity, students practice both listening and speaking skills in a team setting as they brainstorm a solution to this problem: What do you do with inedible gelatin that glows in the dark? Later, they develop guidelines for effective team communication.

OBJECTIVES

The students will

- Define brainstorming
- Use brainstorming to solve a problem
- Analyze the communications dynamic in teamwork
- Develop their thinking skills in a team setting

SETTING THE STAGE

Ask your class to estimate the percentage of time they think people in offices work with others and the percentage of time they work alone. Studies show that people in offices spend more than 70 percent of their time interacting with others. Executives routinely spend more than twenty-six hours per week in meetings, which is one type of communication team.

Today, more people than ever work in teams to do some part of their jobs. You might have students list occupations and situations in which individuals work primarily in teams, such as

- Team sports
- Congressional committees and task forces
- Units of the armed forces
- Actors in a play
- Musicians in a band
- Surgeons and nurses during an operation

PROCEDURE

1. Introduce the brainstorming technique and hand out Sheet 4–1, "Brainstorming Guidelines."
2. Divide the class randomly into teams of five or six students.

21

3. To develop teamwork skills, name one student in each group "observer." This student will not participate in the assignment but will instead sit outside the team and write observations of how the team organizes and functions. He or she will fill out Sheet 4–3, "Team Observation." While the class members should be aware of the task given to the observer, they should not know the questions on the observer's sheet. Emphasize that observers need to be as objective as possible (you may need to define *objective* for the students). The observer's notes will serve as the basis for a discussion to help the class develop guidelines for improving their communication skills.

4. Give team members about five minutes to develop solutions individually using Sheet 4–2, "Redefine a Product." During this time, the observers should familiarize themselves with Sheet 4–3 so they will know what to look for once brainstorming begins.

5. Give the teams fifteen to twenty minutes to brainstorm as directed on the sheet. Tell students not to discuss their ideas with other teams since they will be competing with them to create the best solution.

6. Once team brainstorming is completed, ask each team for its solution, listing each solution on the board. Then conduct a *class* brainstorming session for about five minutes, looking for additional solutions.

7. As a class, decide on the best solution. To determine the best, you might call for

   • A simple show of hands
   • A show of hands to determine the top two, then a second to determine the winner
   • The observers to elect the best

8. Once the winner has been chosen, hand out Sheet 4–4, "Effective Team Communication," and ask each team to identify what helped and what hindered the brainstorming in their team.

9. Use the sheets to discuss with the class the dynamics of team communication. You can begin the discussion by asking what the impact is on the team if

   • A team member does a mediocre job
   • A team member does not like another member
   • A team member does not contribute with enthusiasm

10. Build guidelines for improving team communication skills based on your observers' insights. Some guidelines you might want to include are

- Personal agendas don't help a group do its job.
- A team member should not force his or her ideas on others.
- Too much negative criticism stymies creativity.
- Too little criticism can lead to wasted time spent exploring fruitless paths.
- If you listen well, you can build on other team members' ideas. If you don't listen, the solution can be lost.

The first sheet your observers complete deals with roles people assume on teams. You may want to end your discussion by looking at these roles, which are explored in more depth in the next session.

NOTE ON GRADING

In grading team exercises, consider the following options:

- Give a single grade to the team that reflects the quality of the solution.
- Give a single grade to the team that reflects how well they communicated as a team.
- If a member of a team is clearly not contributing, you can grade this individual separately, but be sure to make this clear ahead of time.
- Grade each member of the team individually, based on his or her contributions to the team assignment. This requires you to concentrate on observing the workings of the groups.
- Have the team members evaluate their own contributions to the success of the team.
- Combine the group and individual grading approaches.

4–1. BRAINSTORMING GUIDELINES

Brainstorming: An open sharing of ideas and suggestions by a group of individuals as they seek solutions to a problem.

The following guidelines should help you brainstorm:

1. Always prepare for the brainstorming session with a few ideas of your own. Do some advance thinking. Consider alternatives the team may explore. You should have something to contribute to the brainstorming session.

2. Don't be afraid to toss out an idea for discussion, no matter how silly it may seem to you. Someone else on the team may see an angle that you don't, build on it, and arrive at the solution. If the idea isn't good, the team will move on.

3. Never penalize a person for contributing an idea, no matter how bad it appears. Finding one good idea often requires exploring twenty bad ones.

4. No one owns an idea! You contribute an idea to the team. A brainstorming session is not a debate where you need to win or score points. Your goal is to arrive at a team solution.

5. Never stop trying, even if others frown at your ideas. You may be on the road to a solution the team hasn't recognized yet.

6. Be open to others' ideas and build on them. Look at alternatives. Add something to someone else's idea.

7. Try not to interrupt a member of the team who is presenting an idea.

8. Hold off being critical until the team has many alternatives to explore. Then rank them from most effective to least effective.

9. Never be afraid of silence. Sometimes everybody on the team needs a minute or two to regain perspective and come up with new ideas. Once you have a new idea, express it.

10. As a member of the team, you must contribute. It's wrong to let others do the work and take credit.

Name _____ Date _____

4–2. REDEFINE A PRODUCT

Directions: Your teacher will divide the class into teams. Assume that your team works for a large company that has a problem to solve. As a team, brainstorm solutions.

THE PROBLEM

Your company has developed a gelatin that glows in the dark. Unfortunately, you produced ten tons of this gelatin before your researchers discovered that if you eat it, it makes you very ill. If you destroy the product, you will go bankrupt. What can you do with ten tons of glow-in-the-dark gelatin that makes people sick?

1. As an individual, list at least three alternative solutions. When the brainstorming session begins, share these ideas with your teammates.

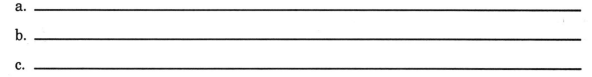

   a. _____

   b. _____

   c. _____

2. As part of your team, brainstorm possible solutions that you believe would make your gelatin marketable.

SOLUTIONS

   a. _____

   b. _____

   c. _____

   d. _____

   e. _____

   f. _____

   g. _____

   h. _____

   i. _____

   j. _____

   k. _____

   l. _____

3. As a group, rank your team's solutions from most effective (1) to least effective (12). Be prepared to give your teacher your team's best solution when called on.

Name _____ Date _____

4–3. TEAM OBSERVATION

Team members: _____

_____

Directions: Your task is to observe and describe, as objectively as possible, how your team works. Review the following questions and answer all of them thoroughly as you sit outside the group and observe it. Take notes on how individuals contribute and what works or does not work. Remember that you cannot become involved in the group's assignment; try not to make the team aware you are there.

TEAM ROLES

1. Did any member of the team become the leader? How did this happen?

   _____

   _____

2. Briefly describe each person's contribution(s) to the completion of the assignment. Avoid passing any judgments. Be objective.

   _____

   _____

   _____

   _____

3. Was participation balanced and equal? If so, how did this happen? If not, why do you think balance was not achieved?

   _____

   _____

4. Did anyone just keep churning out ideas? Was anyone especially creative?

   _____

   _____

5. Did anyone encourage others to contribute ideas? What did he or she typically say?

   _____

   _____

6. Did anyone continually criticize others' ideas? What did he or she typically say?

_____

_____

TEAM PROCESS

7. Was an overall plan for completing the assignment discussed and/or established? If so, who suggested the plan?

_____

8. Was participation in the team's discussion voluntary? Were all members of the team encouraged to participate? If so, how was this done?

_____

_____

9. How was it determined who would actually complete the sheet? Was it the leader or somebody else? Or did everyone keep a separate sheet?

_____

10. When there was a disagreement, how was it resolved?

_____

_____

11. How did the group decide on the best solution? Do you think everyone in the group agreed?

_____

_____

_____

OTHER OBSERVATIONS

In the space beclow, make other notes about what worked and what didn't work in the team's communication.

4–4. EFFECTIVE TEAM COMMUNICATION

Directions: Analyze the interactions that just occurred in your team by answering the following questions as a team.

A. WHAT HELPED: We communicated best as a team when

    1. ＿＿＿＿＿＿＿＿＿＿＿＿＿＿＿＿＿＿＿＿＿＿＿＿＿＿＿＿＿＿＿＿＿＿＿＿

    2. ＿＿＿＿＿＿＿＿＿＿＿＿＿＿＿＿＿＿＿＿＿＿＿＿＿＿＿＿＿＿＿＿＿＿＿＿

    3. ＿＿＿＿＿＿＿＿＿＿＿＿＿＿＿＿＿＿＿＿＿＿＿＿＿＿＿＿＿＿＿＿＿＿＿＿

    4. ＿＿＿＿＿＿＿＿＿＿＿＿＿＿＿＿＿＿＿＿＿＿＿＿＿＿＿＿＿＿＿＿＿＿＿＿

B. WHAT HINDERED: We communicated least effectively as a team when

    1. ＿＿＿＿＿＿＿＿＿＿＿＿＿＿＿＿＿＿＿＿＿＿＿＿＿＿＿＿＿＿＿＿＿＿＿＿

    2. ＿＿＿＿＿＿＿＿＿＿＿＿＿＿＿＿＿＿＿＿＿＿＿＿＿＿＿＿＿＿＿＿＿＿＿＿

    3. ＿＿＿＿＿＿＿＿＿＿＿＿＿＿＿＿＿＿＿＿＿＿＿＿＿＿＿＿＿＿＿＿＿＿＿＿

    4. ＿＿＿＿＿＿＿＿＿＿＿＿＿＿＿＿＿＿＿＿＿＿＿＿＿＿＿＿＿＿＿＿＿＿＿＿

As the other teams share their team experience, add to your team's list:

C. WHAT ELSE MAY HELP: Add suggestions from the other teams.

    1. ＿＿＿＿＿＿＿＿＿＿＿＿＿＿＿＿＿＿＿＿＿＿＿＿＿＿＿＿＿＿＿＿＿＿＿＿

    2. ＿＿＿＿＿＿＿＿＿＿＿＿＿＿＿＿＿＿＿＿＿＿＿＿＿＿＿＿＿＿＿＿＿＿＿＿

    3. ＿＿＿＿＿＿＿＿＿＿＿＿＿＿＿＿＿＿＿＿＿＿＿＿＿＿＿＿＿＿＿＿＿＿＿＿

    4. ＿＿＿＿＿＿＿＿＿＿＿＿＿＿＿＿＿＿＿＿＿＿＿＿＿＿＿＿＿＿＿＿＿＿＿＿

    5. ＿＿＿＿＿＿＿＿＿＿＿＿＿＿＿＿＿＿＿＿＿＿＿＿＿＿＿＿＿＿＿＿＿＿＿＿

D. WHAT ELSE MAY HINDER: Add suggestions from the other teams.

    1. ＿＿＿＿＿＿＿＿＿＿＿＿＿＿＿＿＿＿＿＿＿＿＿＿＿＿＿＿＿＿＿＿＿＿＿＿

    2. ＿＿＿＿＿＿＿＿＿＿＿＿＿＿＿＿＿＿＿＿＿＿＿＿＿＿＿＿＿＿＿＿＿＿＿＿

    3. ＿＿＿＿＿＿＿＿＿＿＿＿＿＿＿＿＿＿＿＿＿＿＿＿＿＿＿＿＿＿＿＿＿＿＿＿

    4. ＿＿＿＿＿＿＿＿＿＿＿＿＿＿＿＿＿＿＿＿＿＿＿＿＿＿＿＿＿＿＿＿＿＿＿＿

    5. ＿＿＿＿＿＿＿＿＿＿＿＿＿＿＿＿＿＿＿＿＿＿＿＿＿＿＿＿＿＿＿＿＿＿＿＿

Session 5. ASSUMING DIFFERENT TEAM ROLES

In this session, students learn about different communication roles that arise in teams. Each student assumes one role in a team for four or five minutes, before being instructed to switch to the next role. Students practice listening, speaking, and thinking skills while observing team interactions from different perspectives.

OBJECTIVES

The students will

- Analyze the different roles people play in teams or groups
- Role play the parts to achieve a team goal
- Practice listening and speaking skills
- Develop thinking skills in a group setting

SETTING THE STAGE

People play different yet distinct roles in teams—just as actors assume different roles in a play on stage. Five basic communication roles are described in Sheet 5–1, "Team Roles."

1. The Nurturer
2. The Critic
3. The Leader
4. The Creative Whiz
5. The Synthesizer

There are other roles in teams (including The Parasite), and it is not uncommon for a person to exchange roles or play many roles within a group. For this session, however, these roles are isolated and frozen. Your students will see that these roles guide their interactions, encouraging certain contributions and prohibiting others.

PROCEDURE

1. Hand out Sheet 5–1, "Team Roles," and discuss the various roles.
2. Break the class into teams of five members, with a different mix than in the last session. Today the teams are assigned the task of developing a slogan for selling the glow-in-the-dark gelatin use that

they voted the best in the previous session. Hand out Sheet 5–2, "Create a Jingle."

3. Before the teams begin brainstorming, assign each member a role. He or she must hold it until instructed to change.

- Each group must have a leader, who will begin the meeting. Assign this role first.
- Assign the role of Creative Whiz to the person to the leader's left.
- Continue assigning roles in the following order for each round:

	1	2	3	4	5
1.	Leader	Whiz	Synthesizer	Nurturer	Critic
2.	Whiz	Leader	Nurturer	Critic	Synthesizer
3.	Nurturer	Critic	Whiz	Synthesizer	Leader
4.	Critic	Synthesizer	Leader	Whiz	Nurturer
5.	Synthesizer	Nurturer	Critic	Leader	Whiz

4. Let students hold each role for about five minutes. When the exercise is complete, ask each group to report their results to the class as a whole.

5. Hand out Sheet 5–3, "Team Member's Self-Evaluation," so students can analyze the experience. When they have completed the sheets, discuss with the class the different roles and what they liked and disliked about each.

5–1. TEAM ROLES

THE NURTURER encourages others; he or she is upbeat about others' contributions. A nurturer might say

- "That's a great idea!"
- "That's good. Let's follow that for a while."
- "Give that idea a chance. Let's explore it."
- "That's wonderful. What a great insight! So now we can . . ."

THE CRITIC quickly anticipates where ideas are headed and ends discussions that are going nowhere. A critic needs to be more thoughtful than negative and must remain focused on the group's objective. It's hard to do this role correctly. A critic might say

- "Wait a minute. I think we're going astray because . . ."
- "That's not going to work because . . ."
- "Let's back up. We're missing the point."

Explaining what is wrong is vital to this role.

THE LEADER orchestrates the group by

- Mediating arguments
- Deciding the order in which people talk
- Cutting off a speaker
- Polling group members who aren't contributing
- Driving the interplay among group members to achieve the objective

The leader does not necessarily have the ultimate vote on issues. He or she should be a neutral referee, keeping the group interaction going.

THE CREATIVE WHIZ keeps churning out ideas. The whiz needs to accept criticism and adapt on the fly. He or she needs to let go of any personal attachment to ideas, instead free-floating as many ideas as possible.

THE SYNTHESIZER listens and puts ideas together. The person in this role does more than just take notes; he or she formulates ideas, provides perspective for the team, and steers the session in new directions. He or she might say

- "Let's stand back and see where we are."
- "Let me see if I have this straight. What we said is . . ."
- "I think if we put everything together, this is what we come up with."

5-2. CREATE A JINGLE

Team members: _____

_____

Directions: As a team, develop a jingle or slogan for the glow-in-the-dark gelatin. Answer the following questions as the team works.

1. What will be the name of your product? Brainstorm alternatives and circle the best.

    a. _____

    b. _____

    c. _____

    d. _____

    e. _____

2. Justify your final choice: _____

    _____

    _____

3. What color do you want the name to be in television commercials and print advertisements? Give four colors and circle the best.

    a. _____   b. _____

    c. _____   d. _____

4. Justify your final choice: _____

    _____

5. Create three taglines (slogans) for the product and then circle the best.

    a. _____

    b. _____

    c. _____

6. Justify your final choice: _____

    _____

    _____

    _____

5–3. TEAM MEMBER'S SELF-EVALUATION

Directions: Immediately following the brainstorming session, answer the following questions about the various roles you assumed.

I. First role: _____

    1. Did it feel natural? _____ Yes _____ No

    2. Did you feel you helped the team in your role? _____ Yes _____ No

    3. What did you like about the role? _____

    _____

    4. What did you dislike? _____

    _____

II. Second role: _____

    1. Did it feel natural? _____ Yes _____ No

    2. Did you feel you helped the team in your role? _____ Yes _____ No

    3. What did you like about the role? _____

    _____

    4. What did you dislike? _____

    _____

III. Third role: _____

    1. Did it feel natural? _____ Yes _____ No

    2. Did you feel you helped the team in your role? _____ Yes _____ No

    3. What did you like about the role? _____

    _____

    4. What did you dislike? _____

    _____

IV. Fourth role: _____

    1. Did it feel natural? _____ Yes _____ No

    2. Did you feel you helped the team in your role? _____ Yes _____ No

    3. What did you like about the role? _____

_____

    4. What did you dislike? _____

_____

V. Fifth role: _____

    1. Did it feel natural? _____ Yes _____ No

    2. Did you feel you helped the team in your role? _____ Yes _____ No

    3. What did you like about the role? _____

_____

    4. What did you dislike? _____

_____

CONCLUSIONS

1. What role did you enjoy the most? Why? _____

_____

_____

_____

2. In which role did you feel you made the greatest contribution to the team? Why? ___

_____

_____

3. Which two roles do you ordinarily assume in a group? _____

_____

Session 6. UNDERSTANDING YOUR AUDIENCE

In this session, students will prepare to work on more formal presentations (written, spoken, or visual) by focusing on the audience and its needs.

OBJECTIVES

The students will

- Learn the importance of the audience
- Analyze possible audiences for specific topics
- Create audience assumption statements

SETTING THE STAGE

To deliver any message effectively, the presenter needs to find common ground with the receiver. Imagine that you want to hand over a lunch tray to someone. Unless you know exactly where that person is located, you may try to hand it over only to see it fall to the floor—the exchange failed to take place. To be an effective communicator, you need to know where your audience is located mentally, or the exchange of information may fail.

Creating an *audience assumption statement* helps you identify the most relevant information about the people you want to receive your message. It should answer one or more of these questions:

- What does the audience want to know?
- What does the audience already know?
- What does the audience currently believe?

PROCEDURE

1. Discuss the importance of audience. Discovering who the audience is sometimes takes detective skills. The presenter needs to dig and pry for facts. Typical questions that might be asked are found on Sheet 6–1, "Identifying the Audience," which you should project or hand out.

2. Divide the class into pairs. Assign one student to be the communicator and the other the host—a person who knows the audience well.

3. Give the communicator Sheet 6–2, "What Do You Know About the Audience?," which will lead to an audience assumption statement.

Give the designated host Sheet 6–3, "Audience Descriptions," which describes various audiences.

4. The communicator asks the host questions and records the answers for three different speaking situations. If a host needs to make up information, it should be recorded on the audience description sheet.

5. The communicator writes audience assumption statements based on answers given by the host.

6. Have students switch roles, this time using Sheet 6–4, "What Do You Know about the Audience?," and Sheet 6–5, "Audience Descriptions."

7. After all students have experienced both roles, compare audience assumption statements with the class as a whole and discuss the kinds of questions students chose to ask. Decide which ones were most useful in extracting relevant information.

8. Collect the exercise sheets, making sure to retain them in pairs. When grading the communicators, check their partners' records for new information that may have changed their understanding of the audience.

6−1. IDENTIFYING THE AUDIENCE

• What do the people in the audience want to know?

• Does the audience have any identifiable attitude toward your subject?

• How large is the audience?

• How familiar are audience members with the subject?

• What is the education level of your audience?

  − Helps you define how much you need to educate

  − Helps define what kind of references you can use

  − Helps determine how sophisticated your communication can be

• Are the audience members required to attend the lecture (or read the work), or are they coming voluntarily?

• What are the jobs of the audience members?

• Where do the audience members live?

6–2. WHAT DO YOU KNOW ABOUT THE AUDIENCE? (A)

Directions: Assume that you are going to make three presentations to three different audiences. You need to learn as much as possible about each audience. For each situation listed below, write four questions (in addition to the one provided for you) that you will ask your partner about the audiences. Record the answers, and then write an audience assumption statement for each situation.

I. You have thirty minutes to tell some workers about the new computers that will be brought into their workplace to change the way they work.

   Question 1. _Are the workers afraid they will lose their jobs?_ _____

   Answer: _____

   Question 2. _____

   Answer: _____

   Question 3. _____

   Answer: _____

   Question 4. _____

   Answer: _____

   Question 5. _____

   Answer: _____

   Audience Assumption Statement: _____

   _____

   _____

II. You must write a one-page description of yourself for a college or job application.

   Question 1. _How many people will be accepted?_ _____

   Answer: _____

   Question 2. _____

   Answer: _____

   Question 3. _____

   Answer: _____

6–2. What Do You Know About the Audience? Continued

Question 4. _____

    Answer: _____

Question 5. _____

    Answer: _____

Audience Assumption Statement: _____

_____

_____

III. You have been asked to provide directions to your school that will be included in a letter.

Question 1. _Can the people who will be coming drive?_ _____

    Answer: _____

Question 2. _____

    Answer: _____

Question 3. _____

    Answer: _____

Question 4. _____

    Answer: _____

Question 5. _____

    Answer: _____

Audience Assumption Statement: _____

_____

_____

Name _____ Date _____

6–3. AUDIENCE DESCRIPTIONS (A)

Directions: Your job is to answer questions. Below, you will find descriptions of three different audiences. Read each one *silently to yourself* and then answer the questions your partner asks about the audience. *Don't* volunteer any information that isn't requested in a question. If you cannot answer a question from the description, make up an answer and note the new information on this sheet. Don't read the description aloud to your partner.

I. Your partner's assignment is to give a thirty-minute presentation to some workers about new computers that will be brought into their workplace and change the way they do their jobs.

> The audience consists of people who have never used computers before. Most don't like the idea of computers because they think they take jobs away from people. They know very little about computers and have never really seen one being used. Sixty people will attend. They don't really want to be there— they were ordered to attend by their employers. They all live in the same city. Everyone has finished high school, but none has gone to college. Nobody will lose a job, but they all will have to change their work habits.

II. Your partner's assignment is to write a one-page description of himself or herself for a college (or job) application.

> The audience consists of a screening committee of three well-educated people who live in a different state from the writer. They all have college degrees. They have to review 250 essays in three days and select the ten most effective essays.

III. Your partner's assignment is to provide directions to your school that will be included in a letter.

> The audience consists of twenty-two parents who are planning to send their children to the United States to attend school for one year and want to consider your school. They live high in the hills of Tibet. They have seen buses and trains in the local village. They are between twenty-four and thirty-seven years of age. They are well educated but have a limited ability to read English.

6–4. WHAT DO YOU KNOW ABOUT THE AUDIENCE? (B)

Directions: Assume that you are going to make three presentations to three different audiences. You need to learn as much as possible about each audience. For each situation listed below, write four questions (in addition to the one provided for you) that you will ask your partner about the audiences. Record the answers, and then write an audience assumption statement for each situation.

I. You have fifteen minutes to try to convince a group of people to vote in favor of a tax increase that will allow the addition of an indoor swimming pool to your school.

    Question 1. _Is the audience mostly parents?_ _____

        Answer: _____

    Question 2. _____

        Answer: _____

    Question 3. _____

        Answer: _____

    Question 4. _____

        Answer: _____

    Question 5. _____

        Answer: _____

    Audience Assumption Statement: _____

    _____

    _____

II. You must write a one-page summary of what you plan to do this summer as part of a contest you want to enter. The contest offers a trip to Europe as the grand prize.

    Question 1. _How old are the judges?_ _____

        Answer: _____

    Question 2. _____

        Answer: _____

    Question 3. _____

        Answer: _____

Question 4. _____

    Answer: _____

Question 5. _____

    Answer: _____

Audience Assumption Statement: _____

_____

_____

III. You have been asked to provide advice about how teenagers and parents can communicate better.

Question 1. _Is there anything special about the parents or teenagers?_ ____

    Answer: _____

Question 2. _____

    Answer: _____

Question 3. _____

    Answer: _____

Question 4. _____

    Answer: _____

Question 5. _____

    Answer: _____

Audience Assumption Statement: _____

_____

_____

6–5. AUDIENCE DESCRIPTIONS (B)

Directions: Your job is to answer questions. Three audiences are described below. Read each description *silently to yourself* and then answer questions your partner asks about each audience. *Don't* volunteer any information that is not requested in a question, and don't read the descriptions aloud to your partner. If you cannot answer a question from the description, make up information and record it on this sheet.

I. Your partner's assignment is to give a fifteen-minute address to a group of people to persuade them to vote in favor of a tax increase that will allow the addition of an indoor swimming pool to your school.

The audience consists of fifty senior citizens at a meeting of the Senior Citizens Bowling League. All of the audience members are retired and living on a fixed income. They are active people and meet twice a week to bowl. They have spent their entire lives in your community, and most of them graduated from your school. In the past, they have been hesitant to support any increase in taxes.

II. Your partner's assignment is to write a one-page summary of what he or she plans to do this summer. The contest offers a trip to Europe as the grand prize.

The audience consists of a committee of five teenagers, each from a different European country, who will visit your country while you visit theirs. They were chosen to be on the committee because they are fluent in English and because they all spend their summers working for the poor and homeless in their countries.

III. Your partner's assignment is to provide advice about how teenagers and parents can communicate better.

The audience consists of a group of thirty parents who moved to this country from other countries about a year ago and are having difficulty with the way that teenagers act in this country. All of them have had at least one of their children arrested for minor crimes, and they are concerned that their children will get into deeper trouble. They speak and read limited English. They meet as a support group every week.

Section 2

Presenting Information Concisely

PRESENTING INFORMATION CONCISELY

Papers cover Kathy Baren's desk—and she must read all of them. She also needs to review two reports, each twenty pages long, for meetings tomorrow. She needs to make important decisions tomorrow that affect people's lives, so she must read the reports. But she has three meetings to attend today and countless phone calls to make. All she has time for is a quick scan to catch important information.

Kathy Baren—and countless others like her—need writers who give their readers

- Only what is needed
- Material packaged for easy accessibility

Session 7. The Need to Be Concise

Students learn why it is important to be concise by answering questions about the messages they receive every day. They also write a short essay that can be used with exercises later in this section.

Session 8. Analyzing Inflated Writing

In this session, students analyze a piece of writing, not for content, but to see how concisely it gets across its ideas.

Session 9. Eliminating Unnecessary Words

One way to make writing more concise is to eliminate unnecessary words. Editing out your own words is difficult at first. In this session, students cross off words from *someone else's* writing.

Session 10. Combining Ideas

A second tactic to make writing more concise is to combine ideas expressed in two or more sentences into one. Again, students first develop their skills by editing someone else's work.

Session 11. Editing for Conciseness

Students apply their new editing skills to make their own writing more concise.

Session 12. Making Text Look Easy to Read

The way information is presented visually plays an important part in communication. Visual elements can clarify ideas and make information more accessible. This session introduces students to visual elements such as bullets, dashes, and space.

Session 13. Headings and Subheadings

Headings and subheadings help readers to

- Obtain a quick idea of the writing
- Quickly find sections appropriate to the task at hand

In this session, students create headings and subheadings for someone else's essay.

Session 14. Using Overviews

Overviews are used increasingly today to make the presentation of information more concise. However, most readers don't know how to use them properly. Few writers know when to use them or how to write them. In this session, students learn when to use them and how to write them.

Session 15. Essay or Bulleted Summary

The techniques students have learned in Section Two provide the basis for a writing format called the *bulleted summary*. This efficient writing format has become common for communicating quickly, especially in the workplace. These exercises introduce students to the bulleted summary format and help them understand when to use it.

Session 16. Mixing Formats

The aim of writing is to make information accessible. Sometimes that means mixing elements of different formats. Thus, writers might use elements from the essay and bulleted summary formats in a single work. In this session, students revise an essay they wrote earlier, combining elements of the essay and the bulleted summary to get information across more effectively.

Session 7. THE NEED TO BE CONCISE

In this session, students consider the importance of being concise in dealing with a typical day's supply of information, and they write a short essay that can be used with exercises later in the session.

OBJECTIVES

The students will

- Analyze the information that bombards them every day
- Analyze the advantages of communicating concisely

SETTING THE STAGE

Sheet 7–1 points out that the information base in our world now doubles every three to four years. In a class discussion, ask the students to consider how this information explosion has impacted workers, e.g., the auto mechanic, sales clerk, police officer, and physician.

PROCEDURE

1. Hand out Sheet 7–1, "The Information Explosion," and have students read its introductory text.
2. Tell your students you want them to analyze what they do every day from a communications perspective. The questions on Sheet 7–1 help the students take an inventory of the messages they process every day. Note that question 5 asks students to write an essay about the need to be concise. Ironically, the essay is not an inherently concise mode of written communication.
3. Discuss with the class the information they process every day and the implications of the information explosion.
4. Once you have graded and returned the essays, collect them again and keep them for possible use in additional sessions in Section Two.

7–1. THE INFORMATION EXPLOSION

Directions: Read the short essay below, and then answer questions 1 through 4. Based on those answers, write an answer to question 5.

From the moment humankind first started recording experiences in writing until the beginning of the twentieth century, information grew at a slow pace. In 1700, an educated man could assemble a small library in a single room to house most of the information available worldwide—and in his lifetime, he could read it all.

Information grew relatively slowly until the 1950s, when practical computer technology began to evolve. Suddenly, the growth rate of information increased dramatically. As a result, many new fields of specialized study were created. The Age of Information was born.

Today, the information base in our world doubles about every three to four years. It has become increasingly difficult to keep up with information, even in a specialized field. It simply takes too long to read all the available information.

Meanwhile, we are also being bombarded with information from countless sources trying to get us to do something: television and radio commercials, junk mail, billboards, headlines, traffic signs, bumper stickers, even T-shirts.

We also deal with many people every day. Teachers, parents, friends, coaches, bosses, customers—all throw information at us.

How can we handle it?

1. List where messages come from during a typical day in your life, both in and out of school. Then estimate the number of messages sent to you from each source each day. For instance, how many television commercials do you see each day?

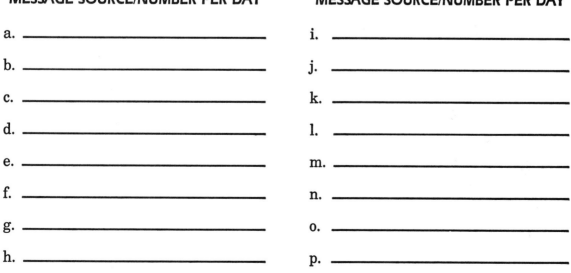

MESSAGE SOURCE/NUMBER PER DAY

a. _____

b. _____

c. _____

d. _____

e. _____

f. _____

g. _____

h. _____

MESSAGE SOURCE/NUMBER PER DAY

i. _____

j. _____

k. _____

l. _____

m. _____

n. _____

o. _____

p. _____

7–1. The Information Explosion Continued

2. Add up the number of messages. How many messages each day try to persuade you to do something? _____

3. Do you think that the amount of information you must handle will grow smaller or larger as you grow older? Support your answer. _____

_____

_____

_____

_____

_____

4. Do you think the amount of information coming from people you deal with on a daily basis will grow smaller or larger as you grow older? Support your answer. _____

_____

_____

_____

_____

5. Assume you are dealing with someone who writes very long answers. You can't handle all the information because you are busy dealing with other problems. On a separate piece of lined paper, write a short essay (200 to 300 words) to persuade the writer to be more concise. Include an argument about the amount of other information you must handle in a single day.

Session 8. ANALYZING INFLATED WRITING

In this session, students grade a traditional essay that is wordy and identify the key ideas obscured by verbosity.

OBJECTIVES

The students will

- Judge the effectiveness of a sample essay
- Identify the key ideas in an essay

SETTING THE STAGE

The previous session demonstrated to students the need for conciseness. In this session, students have to read someone's inflated prose. They discover that the writer's ideas have merit, but digging them out is painful.

Allowing students to become the teacher gives them an objectivity they may not exhibit yet in judging their own work. This shifts the onus of "you're a poor writer" from their shoulders and lets them develop editing skills by judging someone else's work. Later, they'll be able to transfer these skills to their own writing.

PROCEDURE

1. Explain to the class that each student is to become a teacher and grade someone on how concisely ideas are expressed.
2. Hand out Sheet 8–1, "Fingerprinting beyond Fingers," and Sheet 8–2, "Evaluating an Essay." Ask your students to read the essay and grade it on Sheet 8–2 after answering the questions. Explain that *what* is being said is not important, but rather *how* it is expressed. The student's own grade for this assignment depends on that assessment.
3. Students will probably give the essay a low grade because it buries information under many words and extraneous thoughts. Discuss with the class how to improve the work. You might want to

   - Write the essay's essential ideas on the board, or
   - Ask your students to cross out unnecessary words in the essay.

4. When the work is complete, tell students that they have been developing skills that will enable them to make their own writing more concise.

8–1. FINGERPRINTING BEYOND FINGERS

Directions: Assume that you are a teacher who has assigned the writer of this piece to explain the use of fingerprints in modern law enforcement. This is what the student writer turned in to you for evaluation and grading. Read the essay, then respond to the questions on 8–2.

I have been asked to explain the use of fingerprints in law enforcement. I feel it is important that you should be advised that there are many and various reasons for calling to your attention the matter discussed herein.

Fingerprints (which are made by stamping a person's finger in ink and pressing it on a paper) have for many years been used by law enforcement agencies in governments throughout the world to identify people who have committed heinous and also minor crimes. You see, all of the time, a person's fingerprints identify only him and no one else. By that I mean to say that fingerprints uniquely identify a person and no one else. Two people just can't have the same fingerprints. There always will be differences in their fingerprints.

Today, if law enforcement officials find fingerprints at the scene of a crime, they can track down the criminal not only in this country, but also around the world. They use a computer today that is hooked up to other computers around the world to track the criminal down by finding out to whom the fingerprints belong. The computer can match fingerprints with criminals around the world faster than a human could check just the fingerprints in one community.

But what is really different today, and what you should know about, is that any part of a person's body left at the scene of a crime can identify the criminal through what's now called the "biotic fingerprint." That's because whatever is left (it could be a strand of hair or a piece of fingernail or spot of blood) contains DNA of the person. DNA is the genetic material that makes each person a unique individual, different from everybody else. Because everybody's DNA is different from everybody else's DNA, experts can identify a criminal by comparing the DNA left at the crime to a suspect's DNA.

Life is changing very fast, and such is also the case in law enforcement. Fingerprinting is really too narrow a term to use today. We should call it body printing.

Name _____   Date _____

8–2. EVALUATING AN ESSAY

Directions: In this exercise, you are the teacher. Read Sheet 8–1, "Fingerprinting Beyond Fingers," and then answer the questions below to evaluate and grade this piece of writing. Be prepared to discuss your evaluation with the class.

1. List the ideas the writer is trying to get across. You may not need to use every line.

   a. _____

   b. _____

   c. _____

   d. _____

2. Evaluate the essay by circling the term that comes closest to your opinion for each of these areas:

QUALITY OF WRITING:	Poor	Weak	Fair	Good	Excellent
CLARITY OF CONSTRUCTION:	Poor	Weak	Fair	Good	Excellent

3. Cite three major weaknesses of this writing:

   a. _____

   b. _____

   c. _____

4. Suggest two ways to shorten the essay:

   a. _____

   b. _____

5. Considering the evaluations in the previous questions and any other criteria you may wish to use, circle your overall grade for the work:

   A   B   C   D   F

6. Give a specific piece of advice to the writer for revising the work:

   _____

   _____

   _____

   _____

   _____

Session 9. ELIMINATING UNNECESSARY WORDS

One way to make writing more concise is to eliminate unnecessary words, but revising your own work is difficult at first. In this session, students cross out words from *someone else's* writing. This exercise is based on the old adage,

> "No human urge—neither seeking shelter, nor food—is greater than the urge to edit another's copy."

OBJECTIVES

The students will

- Evaluate a wordy essay
- Develop editing skills by removing unnecessary words

SETTING THE STAGE

In the previous session, students learned that it is irritating when too many words interfere with the message. They also saw that extraneous words make extracting meaning more difficult. You might begin this session by telling students that Abraham Lincoln once apologized for the long speech he was about to deliver—he said he didn't have time to write a short one.

PROCEDURE

1. Remind students that a writer should not expect a reader to search for ideas buried in too many words. Writers should strive to eliminate as many words as possible. Share the Lincoln story (above) with your students.
2. Hand out Sheet 9–1, "How Many Words Can You Eliminate?," and tell the students they are assigned to make the writing more accessible by eliminating words—*without* losing any important ideas or information. Their grade depends on how much they can eliminate *without* sacrificing content.
3. After you have graded their work, read some of the best aloud. The class will hear some of the better ways to express the material and learn that there is no "one right way."

ANSWER

One way to edit the work is shown below. Text to eliminate is shown in brackets [ ].

Although [you may find it kind of] hard to imagine today, education [basically] was [a special privilege] reserved [just] for children of wealthy families for thousands [and thousands] of years. Most families lived on farms and needed their children [around] to help with chores. [Thus few children went to school.] Besides, [a family needed to make a whole lot of money before a child could go to school because] the family had to pay for the child's education. But that [traditional educational circumstance, that we find so peculiar,] changed in America in the 1820s. [About that time,] Boston was a growing city, but it didn't have enough people who knew how to read or write or perform arithmetic. [How did Boston solve the problem?] In 1823, Boston opened [up] the [very] first public grammar school, a school that anyone could attend without paying [a single dollar]. When most Americans [throughout the country on average] couldn't read or write [stuff], [just] a [simple] grammar school education was considered [by just about everyone] more than [overly] sufficient [for most all kids]. [But you see,] that still wasn't fair [overall]. After graduating from a grammar school, a few wealthy kids [had money from their folks and they] went on to college. To open [up some] opportunities for [some of the] talented kids from [those] families that were not rich, Boston [then] funded "the people's college," which came to be known as the "high school."

9–1. HOW MANY WORDS CAN YOU ELIMINATE?

Directions: Read the following paragraph all the way through. Then go back through the paragraph and cross out as many words as you can without destroying the meaning. You must leave complete sentences, but you may eliminate any sentences or parts of sentences that are unnecessary.

Although you may find it kind of hard to imagine today, education basically was a special privilege reserved just for children of wealthy families for thousands and thousands of years. Most families lived on farms and needed their children around to help with chores. Thus few children went to school. Besides, a family needed to make a whole lot of money before a child could go to school because the family had to pay for the child's education. But that traditional educational circumstance, that we find so peculiar, changed in America in the 1820s. About that time, Boston was a growing city, but it didn't have enough people who knew how to read or write or perform arithmetic. How did Boston solve the problem? In 1823, Boston opened up the very first public grammar school, a school that anyone could attend without paying a single dollar. When most Americans throughout the country on average couldn't read or write stuff, just a simple grammar school education was considered by just about everyone more than overly sufficient for most all kids. But you see, that still wasn't fair overall. After graduating from a grammar school, a few wealthy kids had money from their folks and they went on to college. To open up some opportunities for some of the talented kids from those families that were not rich, Boston then funded "the people's college," which came to be known as the "high school."

© 1992 by The Center for Applied Research in Education

Session 10. COMBINING IDEAS

A second tactic to make writing more concise is to combine ideas expressed in two or more sentences into one. Note that this exercise can be easily transferred to a word processor and edited on disk by the students.

OBJECTIVES

The students will

- Analyze wordy paragraphs
- Combine ideas to make the paragraphs more concise

SETTING THE STAGE

Combining ideas can make writing more concise, as well as more specific and focused. What are the clues to combining ideas? Look for *substitutions*. Do phrases from two sentences mean exactly the same thing? Can they be combined into one sentence? Can one be eliminated?

PROCEDURE

1. Share with students the preceding suggestions for uncovering unnecessary phrases and sentences.
2. Hand out the Sheet 10–1, "How Many Ideas Can You Combine?." Tell the class they are to combine ideas to make the paragraphs more concise *without* losing any important ideas or information. Their grade depends on how much they can eliminate without sacrificing content.
3. After you have evaluated their work, read some of the best aloud and ask students to explain why they made their revisions.

ANSWERS

1. *Founded in 1986, the company offered a low-cost container.*
   Logic: "At that time" is the same as "1986," so the two elements are combined.
2. *Ed excelled in baseball, football, and volleyball.*
   Logic: "baseball, football, and volleyball" are sports. By replacing "sports" with these, the paragraph becomes more concise and more specific.

3. *Diedre swore that the driver of the other car lost control and hit her.*
   Logic: If the other driver lost control, the accident obviously isn't Diedre's responsibility. Why bring up "responsibility?"

4. *The store was shaded. When the building across the street was torn down, the afternoon sun began to beat down on the store. The store was forced to install an air conditioner. Could the store owner sue the building owner to recover the costs associated with the new air conditioner?*
   Logic: The line "The afternoon sun raised the temperature in the store" was removed because the rise in temperature is clearly implied by the two surrounding sentences.

5. *Founded in 1986, the company offered a low-cost container. In 1988, it added a line of biodegradable containers.*
   Logic: "Adding a line of biodegradable containers" means the same as "expanding the business," but it is more precise. By combining ideas, the paragraph becomes more concise and specific.

© 1992 by The Center for Applied Research in Education

Name _____ Date _____

10-1. HOW MANY IDEAS CAN YOU COMBINE?

Directions: Read each paragraph and combine ideas without destroying meaning. You must leave complete sentences, but you may eliminate any sentences or parts of sentences that you judge unnecessary. You may change or add new words. Be prepared to explain why you made your revisions.

1. The company was founded in 1986. At that time, it offered a low-cost container.

   _____

2. Ed excelled in sports. He played not only baseball, but also football and volleyball.

   _____

   _____

3. Diedre denied responsibility for the accident. She swore that the driver of the other car lost control and hit her.

   _____

   _____

4. The store was shaded. When the building across the street was torn down, the afternoon sun began to beat down on the store. The afternoon sun raised the temperature in the store. The store was forced to install an air conditioner. Can the store owner sue the building owner to recover the costs associated with the new air conditioner?

   _____

   _____

   _____

5. The company was founded in 1986. At that time, it offered a low-cost container. In 1988, the company expanded its business. In addition to the low-cost container, it also offered a biodegradable line of containers. (*Hint:* Use your answer to question 1 as a start.)

   _____

   _____

   _____

Session 11. EDITING FOR CONCISENESS

In this session, students apply their new editing skills to make their *own* writing more concise.

OBJECTIVE

The students will create a work and make it more concise through editing.

SETTING THE STAGE

Since students have worked on presenting information concisely in the last four sessions, it is important to remind them to let themselves go in the first draft. Remind them that conciseness is not as important in the first draft as creating ideas—nor should they be overly concerned with spelling, grammar, or organization. But creating ideas is just the beginning. The writing process continues. Once they know what they want to say, they can work on getting it across by making it more concise.

PROCEDURE

1. Ask the class if there is much difference between reworking their own writing and someone else's. Reworking your own is usually much more difficult because you have to distance yourself from what you're trying to say and gauge how the audience will receive it.

2. Pass out Sheet 11–1, "First Draft: In the Future," and ask the class to write a short essay about the future as instructed. You might want to brainstorm with the class for future changes to add to the list of topics. The brainstorming itself should help to interest students in the assignment. *As an alternative*, you might want to pass out the essays students wrote in Session 7 about being concise and use them instead.

3. Remind students that in first drafts they should not be concerned about being concise or mechanically correct.

4. When students have finished, pass out Sheet 11–2, "Editing Your Own Work." They should cut words or phrases in their first draft with a single line, so you can read what was crossed off. Then they should rewrite the essay as an editor would—combining ideas and trimming fat without removing any important ideas (or adding any new ideas).

5. Collect the work. Grade the students on how concisely they present their information. You can write notes about the quality of their thinking about the future, but their grades should be based solely on how concisely the information is conveyed.

Name _____   Date _____

11–1. FIRST DRAFT: IN THE FUTURE

Directions: On the front (and, if necessary, back) of this sheet, write the first draft of a personal essay of approximately 300 words, describing how one of the following changes might affect your future life.

- Household robots
- A space station
- Voice-activated typewriters/word processors
- A worldwide oil shortage
- Or any other probable change, as long as your teacher agrees

_____

_____

_____

_____

_____

_____

_____

_____

_____

_____

_____

_____

_____

_____

_____

_____

_____

_____

Name _____   Date _____

11−2. EDITING YOUR OWN WORK

Directions: Go back over the short essay you wrote about the future and cross out as many ideas as you can without destroying the overall meaning of the work. Use a single line to cross out ideas so your teacher can see what you cut. Combine ideas when possible. You must leave complete sentences, but you may eliminate any sentences or parts of sentences that are unnecessary. Next, rewrite your essay in the space below, reducing it to 150 words without dropping any main ideas. To accomplish this, consider combining ideas and eliminating unnecessary descriptive terms.

Session 12. MAKING TEXT LOOK EASY TO READ

Although easy to overlook, the visual presentation of information plays an important role in communication. Visual elements can save words, clarify ideas, and make information more accessible. This session's exercise introduces students to visual elements in writing such as space, bullets, and dashes. These activities work particularly well on a word processor. If you transfer them to a disk, students will be able to concentrate on visual elements without needing to copy the entire text.

OBJECTIVES

The students will

- Recognize visual elements available to writers
- Use visual elements to help convey information

SETTING THE STAGE

Jim Faxton needs to read a 75-page report tonight. Page 3 is one long solid paragraph. It looks so uninviting that he skips the page completely!

Had the writer of the 75-page report taken the time to break the long paragraph into smaller paragraphs with white space between them, Jim Faxton would have found the material inviting enough at least to skim, not skip.

Visual elements make information more accessible for the reader, speeding along the flow of information. You and your students can immediately gauge the effect of visual elements by comparing the two versions of the same text on Sheet 12–1, "Visual Guidelines: Two Examples." Which would you rather read? Which would you want for reference when you had a question?

Listing information presents a special question. How do you *punctuate* the end of a bulleted point (or numbered point, etc.)? Use a period if the bulleted text is a complete sentence. If it is a fragment, use no punctuation, not even for the last fragment in the list. A period is used to indicate an end to the idea, but the fragment's position on the list already serves that purpose, making the period unnecessary.

PROCEDURE

1. Hand out Sheet 12–1, "Visual Guidelines: Two Examples." Ask your class which text they would rather read, and discuss the visual elements that make the second version more appealing:

   • Indenting and outdenting
   • White space, extra space between paragraphs
   • Numbering fragments, sentences, or entire paragraphs
   • Bulleting elements (or using dashes or asterisks)
   • Italicizing and boldfacing text

2. On Sheet 12–2, "Using Visual Elements," students can use a number of visual elements. Note that when lists are used, all list elements are parallel in construction. This is important, because if they are not parallel, readers must slow down and decode them.

3. For extra work on this topic, return the essays the students wrote about the future or about being concise and have them rewrite using visual elements.

ANSWERS

Many possibilities will be acceptable; one solution is given here for numbers 1 and 2. A possible solution for number 4 is on Sheet 12–3, which you can project or distribute.

1. To get cash from the 24-hour teller at the bank, you must

   1. Insert your passcard.
   2. Enter your passcode.
   3. Identify whether you want the money from

      • checking
      • savings
      • credit card

   4. Specify how much money you want.

2. The out-of-court settlement benefited both parties:

   • Jackson gained the property he sought.
   • Adams gained the money he sought.

12–1. VISUAL GUIDELINES: TWO EXAMPLES

EXAMPLE 1

Visual elements enable the reader to scan materials to identify important points with ease. For readers, material is easier to read when it incorporates visual elements. For example, a long paragraph may look like a large wall to a reader—a daunting sight. Breaking the paragraph into smaller paragraphs makes the same material look like hurdles that can be easily jumped. Adding space between paragraphs opens up the look of the presentation, making it appear even less difficult. To call attention to a new idea, the first line of a paragraph can be indented. Indenting all lines in blocks of ideas (as done in outlining) can be used to help the reader quickly see relationships among ideas. As an alternative, "outdenting" can be used to draw attention to new ideas. In outdenting, the first line of a paragraph begins at the margin and subsequent lines are indented. It is important, however, that the first line of the paragraph contain the major idea when outdenting. Instead of running a series of ideas or pieces of information together in a sentence, they can be placed in a list with a symbol preceding each item. Common list symbols include numbers, bullets, asterisks, and dashes. Use numbers when the order of the items is important. Use bullets, asterisks, or dashes when the order of presentation is not significant. In listings, capitalize the first word of each item in the list to add emphasis to the item. Also, capitalize all important words in headings and subheadings to draw attention to these words. You can also call attention to key words and important thoughts by underlining them. Underlined thoughts would be printed in italics by a professional printer. Boldface, a part of most word processing packages, is usually reserved for headings and titles, but it may also be used to call attention to something the reader should not miss. A squiggly line under words indicates that they should be printed in boldface.

EXAMPLE 2

Visual elements enable the reader to scan materials to identify important points with ease.

For readers, material is easier to read when it incorporates visual elements. For example, a long paragraph may look like a large wall to a reader—a daunting sight. Breaking the paragraph into smaller paragraphs makes the same material look like hurdles that can be easily jumped.

White Space

Adding space between paragraphs opens up the look of the presentation, making it appear even less difficult.

Indenting and Outdenting

To call attention to a new idea, the first line of a paragraph can be indented.

Indenting all lines in blocks of ideas (as done in outlining) can be used to help the reader quickly see relationships among ideas.

12–1. Visual Guidelines: Two Examples Continued

Outdenting also draws attention to new ideas. In outdenting, the first line of a paragraph
begins at the margin and subsequent lines are indented. It is important, however,
that the first line of the paragraph contain the major idea when outdenting.

Listing

A series of ideas or pieces of information could get lost in a continuously flowing sentence
or paragraph. You can call attention to them by displaying them in a list with a symbol
preceding each item. Common list symbols include

1. Numbers
- Bullets
* Asterisks
– Dashes

Use numbers when the order of the items is important. Use bullets, asterisks, or dashes
when the order is not important.

Capital Letters

Capitalize all important words in headings and subheadings to draw attention to those
words. In listings, capitalize the first word of each item.

Underlining, Italics, and Boldface

You can also call attention to key words and important thoughts by underlining them.

Underlined thoughts would be printed in *italics* by a professional printer. **Boldface**, a

part of most word processing packages, is usually reserved for headings and titles, but

it may also be used to call attention to something the reader should not miss.

A squiggly line under words indicates boldface.

© 1992 by The Center for Applied Research in Education

12–2. USING VISUAL ELEMENTS

Directions: On a separate sheet of paper, rewrite each of the following, using visual elements (white space, headings, indents, lists, etc.) to emphasize the information presented. Do not omit any information.

1. To get cash from the 24-hour teller at the bank, you must insert your passcard; enter your passcode; identify whether you want the money from checking, savings, or credit card; and specify how much money you want.

2. The out-of-court settlement benefited both parties: Jackson gained the property he sought and Adams gained the money he sought.

3. Preparing for the job interview can be the key to your success. Learn as much as you can about the company so that you can ask intelligent questions and show that you are really interested in them. Dress in appropriate clothes—neat, clean, and conservative. Be certain to be punctual and try to avoid showing how nervous you are. Wringing your hands, swaying your legs, wiggling in your seat, or playing with a piece of jewelry you are wearing will give away your nervousness. And above all, try to smile.

4. In the early 1920s, radio broadcasters discovered they could pull money out of the air, something they had never done before.

   Marconi invented the radio in the late 1800s. But for decades, no one knew what to do with it. Some people thought it might someday be used as a wireless telephone. Others thought it would only be used for ship-to-shore communication. A few hobbyists used it to talk to one another.

   In the 1920s, a realtor paid a radio hobbyist to tell listeners about an apartment he was selling in New York City. That changed the history of radio. More people came to look at the apartment than the realtor had ever expected. Word spread.

   Soon stores were paying to broadcast commercials about sales, and their stores were flooded with people from miles away. The radio broadcasters were "pulling money from the air."

   People began buying radios. Broadcasters started playing music and offering other entertainment to attract listeners, so more people could hear the commercials. With the allure of entertainment, more people bought radios. A new industry was born, and radio flourished.

12–3. THE BEGINNING OF RADIO

In the early 1920s, radio broadcasters discovered they could pull money out of the air—something they had never done before.

* Marconi invented the radio in the late 1800s, but for decades, no one knew what to do with it.

   – Some people thought it might someday be used as a wireless telephone.

   – Others thought it would only be used for ship-to-shore communication.

   – A few hobbyists used it to talk to one another.

* In the 1920s, a realtor paid a radio hobbyist to tell listeners about an apartment he was selling in New York City. That changed the history of radio.

   – More people came to look at the apartment than the realtor had ever expected.

   – Word spread.

* Soon stores were paying to broadcast commercials about sales, and their stores were flooded with people from miles away. The radio broadcasters were "pulling money from the air."

* People began buying radios. Broadcasters started playing music and offering other entertainment to attract listeners, so more people could hear the commercials. With the allure of entertainment, more people bought radios.

   – A new industry was born, and radio flourished.

Session 13. USING HEADINGS AND SUBHEADINGS

When readers must find information quickly, the writer needs to help. Headings and subheadings enable a reader to obtain an overview of the content and quickly find those sections that are relevant to the task at hand.

In this session, students create headings and subheadings for someone else's essay. Since they do not have to write the text, they can focus on the headings. This is a good exercise to do on a word processor.

OBJECTIVES

The students will

- Understand the purpose of headings and subheadings
- Develop parallel headings and subheadings

SETTING THE STAGE

Assume you have a 100-page report to read. You know that of those 100 pages, only a small part of the information is relevant to you. It's a waste of time and energy to read all the material. Headings and subheadings can help you locate the information you need. As a writer, you make your information more accessible to the reader if you provide headings and subheadings.

PROCEDURE

1. Discuss with your class the need for headings and subheadings.
2. Hand out Sheet 13–1, "Headings and Subheadings," and go over what headings and subheadings are, how to create them, and the rules for using them.
3. Hand out Sheet 13–2, "Using Headings and Subheadings," which asks students to write and insert headings and subheadings in an essay on education in ancient Rome.
4. If you grade Sheet 13–2, you should consider
   - Where headings and subheadings are placed
   - How they are expressed (whether they are parallel)
   - How they appear visually (consistent, effective use of visual elements)

ANSWERS

Headings for the essay will vary, but might include

Education for a Poor Child
Education for a Privileged Child

Subheadings under "Education for a Privileged Child" might include

An Elementary Education
Grammar School
Rhetoric School
Higher Learning

Alternative subheadings might include

Ages 7–12
Ages 12–15
Ages 15–20
Schooling in Later Years

13–1. HEADINGS AND SUBHEADINGS

WHAT ARE HEADINGS AND SUBHEADINGS?

HEADINGS divide large blocks of text by topic. SUBHEADINGS subdivide these blocks into smaller units—subtopics within topics.

HOW DO I KNOW WHEN TO USE THEM?

To create headings,

1. Review the entire work.
2. Note paragraphs where the subject matter changes.
3. Determine the main subject matter of each block of text.
4. Create a short heading to convey the subject matter.

Use the same process to review each block and determine if and where subheadings are warranted.

WHAT DO I NEED TO KNOW ABOUT USING THEM PROPERLY?

1. You should not use a single heading in a work. If you only have one heading, make it the title. At least two headings are required, but you can create as many as you like. Likewise, you need at least two subheadings in each section of the material if you are going to have subheadings at all.
2. All headings in a work should be grammatically parallel. For instance, if you use a sentence fragment for the first heading, all other headings must also be fragments that follow the same pattern. For example, note that all the headings on this sheet are in a question format. Before writing a heading, make sure the format you have chosen works throughout the piece.
3. All subheadings within a section should also be grammatically parallel to each other.
4. Headings and subheadings need not, however, be grammatically parallel to each other. Often, making them different helps the reader distinguish one from the other. For example,

Heading:	The Bulleted Summary
Subheadings:	Using Lists for Simplification
	Using Space for Emphasis

5. If possible, use additional visual elements to distinguish headings from subheadings (with headings looking more important than subheadings). Some of the elements you can use include CAPITAL LETTERS, underlining, **bold print**, or larger print. Make sure whatever visual elements you choose are used consistently.

13–2. USING HEADINGS AND SUBHEADINGS

Directions: Read the following essay about education in ancient Rome. Then complete both of these assignments:

A. The essay starts with a brief introductory paragraph in which two basic ideas are presented. Analyze the essay to identify these two ideas. Put a check next to the paragraph where each one of these ideas is *first* presented. Then create a brief heading for each block and write it next to your check. Make sure that the headings are parallel in both grammar and format. When you're done, you will have two headings.

B. Review the block of information about education available to children from privileged homes. This block can be divided into four subblocks. Review the block and determine the main idea in these four subsections. Put a check next to where each subblock begins. Create subheadings for these subblocks and write them next to your checks. Make sure your four subheadings are also parallel in both grammar and format.

AN ANCIENT ROMAN EDUCATION

Schools in Ancient Rome were unlike the schools we have today. The Romans did not have public schools that all children could attend. The type of education you received depended on the wealth of your parents.

The parents of most children did not have the money for their children's education, and so these children learned by watching their parents. The son of a craftsman watched his father make pottery. The son of a farmer learned by watching and helping his father in the field. A daughter learned by helping her mother with household chores. Mothers taught most of these children to read, write, and perform basic math.

The education of a child from a privileged home was quite different. If a child's parents had money for education, how far the child went in school was usually determined by how much money the parents had.

An elementary education was available to all children, ages seven to twelve, whose parents had even small amounts of money for education. Their parents would contract with a teacher to instruct the basic skills. The quality of the education was inconsistent because it was determined by how much the parent spent. Anyone could become a teacher, regardless of his education.

13–2. Using Headings and Subheadings Continued

All someone had to do to become an elementary teacher was pitch a tent in the marketplace and begin hawking the school. These tents were set up right next to merchants selling their wares, yelling for attention. The classroom might be curtained off, but it was still very distracting for students.

Within the classroom, children of all ages were mixed together. The teacher called them to his desk one at a time for individual instruction, although sometimes they did engage in competitive, group lessons. Graduating from the elementary school was determined by the student mastering the basic skills, not by the age of the student.

When students left elementary school, they went on to a grammar school if the parents could afford it. Grammar school generally served children ages twelve to fifteen. At a grammar school, students learned literature and grammar. They read a well-defined set of classics. Grammar school was the maximum education for a girl in ancient Rome. Grammar school teachers had better educations than elementary school teachers, but they had to negotiate with parents, too.

Completing grammar school study, a wealthy Roman boy entered the rhetoric school, where he might stay from ages fifteen to twenty. In the rhetoric school, the boy aimed to master public speaking or oratory. Public speaking was a highy regarded and necessary skill for men in public life. In an age before television or newspapers, public opinion was shaped by public speaking.

The student learned the Roman rhetorical tradition and practiced speaking. The teachers won fame for their own oratorical skills, and their fame attracted students. These teachers taught in buildings, far from the marketplace. This education was very expensive. Rhetoric school ended the education for most young men.

Further education was available. If a student had the ability, and his parents had the money, he could go on to study law, medicine, or philosophy. He could enter a law school, a Roman innovation, which was much like ours today, or he could study medicine with a doctor, where he basically became an apprentice. He might also study with a philosopher, although very few students took this course.

Session 14. USING OVERVIEWS

An overview is an introductory paragraph that summarizes the key ideas or key topics that follow. It helps a reader (or a listener) decide whether information is pertinent to the task at hand; it also helps a reader or listener better understand what follows by providing a framework.

Overviews are increasingly used today; however, many readers don't know how to use them properly. Likewise, few writers know when to use them or how to write them.

OBJECTIVES

The students will

- Define *overview*
- Learn the purpose of overviews
- Create an overview

SETTING THE STAGE

With so much information in the world, we cannot always read all the way through a piece of writing to see whether it deals with ideas or topics of interest to us. An overview can help us decide whether to invest the time in reading.

In this book, each section begins with an overview so you can quickly decide if you want to look more closely at a given session. Student textbooks often contain overviews and might prove to be useful examples.

PROCEDURE

1. Hand out Sheet 14–1, "The Overview," which defines overviews and offers guidelines for creating them. Discuss the material with your class, especially

   - When to use an overview as a writer
   - How to use an overview as a reader

2. Hand out Sheet 14–2, "Writing an Overview." Tell your students they are proposing an activity to raise funds for seriously ill children. The audience is a committee of adults. A great deal of thinking and writing has already been done on the details of the activity. Now, students must write the overview.

3. Discuss with the class what the overview must accomplish. Assume that the committee receives a lot of proposals and only has time to read those in which it is most interested. By looking at the first few lines, committee members can immediately know what the proposal is about, without getting bogged down in details like the exact time and date of the proposed car wash.

4. Ask students to follow instructions on Sheet 14–2 to write the overview.

5. If you plan to grade the work, consider how well the students identify key points and express them in the overview.

6. Consider putting students into teams after they have written their individual overviews. Ask each team to write an overview, using the best from each individual effort.

ANSWER

Answers will vary, but one solution is the following:

"We propose to hold a car wash in early September to raise money for seriously ill children. The funds can buy pajamas, books, toys, and other items not covered by medical insurance."

14–1. THE OVERVIEW

An overview is a summary of the key concepts or topics that immediately follow.

PURPOSE

To a reader, an overview is valuable because it provides an instant orientation to new material. By reading this overview, the reader decides whether the material is pertinent to the task at hand.

An overview presents broad concepts or topics that will be covered, not details. It may also contain information that applies to *all* of the material that follows. This saves the writer from repeating material, and the reader from having to read the same material over and over. However, readers who fail to read such an overview miss valuable information. For example, the overview for a chapter in a technical manual may contain vital information about a special computer command that is relevant to all material in the chapter. *As a reader, you should always read the overview so you do not miss any important information.*

While we usually think of overviews for written work, they can also be used in oral and visual presentations to help the audience follow the material.

GUIDELINES

1. Write the overview *last*. When you are happy with your writing (including the visual elements, headings, and subheadings), start the overview.

2. Underline key phrases in the portion of your writing for which you're preparing an overview. Put these ideas into your overview notes.

3. Look for common information under your subheadings. If you find some, consider putting it in your overview notes and crossing it out of the writing itself, making it even more concise.

4. Organize the material in your notes into sentences. Do not change any important words or phrases. You want the material in the overview to say the exact thing the reader will find in the text. Overviews prepare the reader for what follows; the reader should never be surprised.

5. Quickly scan your overview and see if you skip words. If you skip them, the reader probably will skip them, too. Decide whether these words are necessary for the overview. If not, cross them out to make the overview more concise. If they are necessary, try emphasizing them in new ways—for example, by putting them in a new sentence or paragraph or by making them into bulleted lists.

6. Overviews should contain simple, declarative sentences. Do not try to be stylistically clever. Complex sentence construction slows down a reader. Review your overview and see if you can simplify the sentences.

7. Finally, read the overview and make sure it will make sense the first time someone reads it.

14–2. WRITING AN OVERVIEW

An overview is: _____

_____

_____

Directions: You are in a student group that wants to raise money for seriously ill children. You have to get approval for a project you have planned from a committee that receives a lot of proposals. Committee members, who are all adults, only have time to read those in which they are most interested. An overview will enable them to understand quickly what your proposal is about and whether they want to consider it seriously. Read the full proposal below and then follow the directions to write an overview.

THE PROPOSAL

The Cause: We want to help seriously ill children in our area. We will raise money and turn it over to your committee to buy pajamas, books, and toys for the kids. These items are not covered by medical insurance.

The Activity: A car wash is a popular way to raise money. We need to buy only soap, because we have all the other materials (buckets, hoses, and cloths for drying). We will open the activity to anyone in our school. Six students have already committed their time.

Time and Place: We will hold the car wash the first Saturday in September. Many people return from vacation that weekend and want their cars washed. We will work from 9 in the morning to 3 in the afternoon, when most people drive around to shop. We will hold the car wash in our school yard, where we have held other car washes. The school is well located, so a great deal of traffic goes by.

Advertising: We will make posters to advertise the car wash and its purpose and place them in local malls and shopping centers. The local newspaper has offered us advertising space as a donation to the project.

The Funds: We will designate a treasurer who will be responsible for all funds. The treasurer will turn over the funds to your committee late Saturday afternoon.

Fund Raising Goal: We expect to raise $300. We will charge $5 to wash a car and $7 to wash a van. We need to wash about sixty vehicles, or ten an hour. In past car washes, we have handled more cars.

DIRECTIONS

1. Go back through the proposal and underline key phrases.
2. From those phrases, select *only* the key points you want to emphasize to the committee.

14–2. *Writing an Overview Continued*

3. Combine those points into two or three sentences. Try to use the same words or phrases that appear in the proposal. Write a draft of your overview.

4. Scan the overview. Try to eliminate unnecessary words and combine ideas.

5. Revise your overview and write the final draft below for submission. Remember, keep your overview as short as possible.

YOUR OVERVIEW

_____

_____

_____

_____

_____

_____

Session 15. ESSAY OR BULLETED SUMMARY?

The bulleted summary is a writing format that has become common, especially in the workplace, because it helps the reader locate information quickly. It is not a universal solution to all communication needs; neither is the essay. The following exercises introduce students to the bulleted summary format and help them analyze when to use it.

OBJECTIVES

The students will

- Compare and contrast the essay and bulleted summary
- Analyze the purpose of each format
- Characterize the bulleted summary

SETTING THE STAGE

Rebecca Mathers worked as an intern for a company the summer before her senior year. She did a great job, and a vice president asked her to make a few suggestions for future interns.

Rebecca wrote an essay that she was sure would get an "A" in class. A few days after she handed it over, the vice president sat her down. He advised her to learn to write if she wanted to get ahead. She looked perplexed. He explained that he had wanted a few suggestions. He hadn't expected that it would take so much work to read what she wrote. He confessed that he had never even gotten to the end.

He told her that he wanted her main ideas right up top in a sentence or two, followed by a quick sketch of her ideas. "Don't they teach you to write in school?" he asked. She didn't dare tell him she was a straight "A" student.

The essay, which has served us so well in the academic environment, has proven cumbersome in many other situations. New formats have developed for communicating information quickly, and one of the most common of these formats is the bulleted summary.

The bulleted summary combines all the presentation tactics discussed in this section: visual elements, overviews, headings, and so on. You will find a sample of a bulleted summary on Sheet 15–3, "Bulleted Summary Example: The Crocodile."

PROCEDURE

1. Hand out Sheet 15–1, "Essay Example: The Crocodile," and Sheet 15–2, "Essay Structure and Purpose." Students should read the essay on Sheet 15–1 and then answer the questions on Sheet 15–2 to clarify their understanding of the essay's purpose.

2. When that work is complete, hand out Sheet 15–3, "Bulleted Summary Example: The Crocodile," and Sheet 15–4, "Comparing and Contrasting the Essay and the Bulleted Summary." Sheets 15–2 and 15–3 present exactly the same information in different formats. By answering the questions on Sheet 15–4, students will clarify their understanding of the differences between the two formats.

3. Collect the material and evaluate the work. You will find an answer sheet for Sheet 15–4 on Sheet 15–5, "Differences between the Essay and Bulleted Summary," which can be handed out to students. Tell them to retain it for future reference.

ANSWERS

To Sheet 15–2, "Essay Structure and Purpose":

1. B
2. Sentence revealing purpose: "However, is this reputation fair?"
3. A (through the use of a question, as well as vivid description)
4. D
5. Paragraph 2—physical characteristics
   Paragraph 3—behavior
   Paragraph 4—approaching extinction

15–1. ESSAY EXAMPLE: THE CROCODILE

The crocodile has a reputation for being a vicious, life-threatening danger to humanity. Certainly its lizard-like appearance makes it appear as if it is always ready to attack, and often movies have portrayed these animals as enemies waiting in ambush to turn the unsuspecting human being into an evening snack. However, is this reputation fair?

The physical characteristics of the crocodile present a very negative image. Its long body, which ranges from six to twenty feet, is covered with horny plates that provide protection from other predators. It has short legs that end in clawed, webbed toes, and its long snout contains a very large mouth with razor-sharp, cone-shaped teeth. The major weapons for fighting are its very powerful jaws and a long, massive tail that can knock an enemy unconscious.

The behavior of the crocodile also contributes to its reputation as a danger to humanity. Spending most of its time partly submerged in water, it looks as if it is spying. It can stay this way for long periods of time because its nose, eyes, and ears are high up on its head, allowing it to breathe, see, and hear while mostly under water. The noises it makes can also be frightening, roaring to establish its own territory and hissing in warning. Indeed, the crocodile eats meat, and thus small animals in its territory are in danger of becoming a meal. However, it is rare for a crocodile to attack a human being, and so the crocodile should not be labeled a man-eater.

Crocodiles are found in many parts of the world, mostly in tropical and subtropical climates, and they used to be found in very large numbers. Today, however, they are approaching extinction in many locations where civilization has encroached on their natural habitats. They are often killed because they wander from their natural environments into nearby settlements, thus posing a danger to pets and farm animals. Thousands are also killed each year to provide leather for boots, belts, and luggage. In addition, in some countries, hunting crocodies is a popular sport.

The crocodile is actually a very intelligent animal, capable of being tamed and trained. However, it is a creature of the wild and can be a danger to a human being if it is provoked. But the truth is, the human is a greater danger to the survival of the crocodile than the crocodile is to the human.

15–2. ESSAY STRUCTURE AND PURPOSE

Directions: Read the essay on Sheet 15–1, and then analyze its structure by answering the following questions.

1. Which of the following was most likely the assignment for which this essay was written? Place a check in the blank before your answer. Be prepared to tell why you selected this answer and rejected the other three.

——— a. Describe the physical appearance of the crocodile.

——— b. Discuss the crocodile as a threat to humankind.

——— c. Explain why crocodiles are an endangered species.

——— d. Describe the behavior of the crocodile.

2. The primary purpose of the introductory (or lead) paragraph in an essay is to establish its purpose. Find the statement of purpose in the introductory paragraph, circle it, and write "purpose" in the margin next to it.

3. Another purpose of the introductory paragraph in an essay may be either of the options listed below. Which of these was more likely the goal of the writer of this essay? Place a check in the blank before your answer.

——— a. To gain the reader's desire to read the essay

——— b. To establish that the writer is knowledgeable on the subject

4. How can a writer accomplish the purposes listed in question 3? Which of the common techniques listed below was used in this introductory paragraph? Place a check in the blank before your answer.

——— a. Tell a short anecdote (entertaining fact or story)

——— b. Cite specific, important facts

——— c. Make a startling statement

——— d. Ask a question the reader will want answered

5. Below, copy the phrases in paragraphs 2, 3, and 4 that establish the purpose (or topic) of each of these paragraphs.

Paragraph 2: ——————————————————————————

Paragraph 3: ——————————————————————————

Paragraph 4: ——————————————————————————

6. The final paragraph in the essay is its conclusion, and the primary function of the conclusion is to reemphasize the purpose of the essay. Circle the sentence in the concluding paragraph that restates the purpose of the essay.

15–3. BULLETED SUMMARY EXAMPLE: THE CROCODILE

The crocodile is popularly portrayed as a danger to humanity. But the human is a greater danger to the survival of the crocodile than the crocodile is to the human being.

POSSIBLE EXTINCTION

- Encroachment on their natural habitats by civilization
- Use of skins for leather for boots, belts, and luggage
- Hunting of crocodiles a popular sport in some countries

POPULAR IMAGE

A reputation as a vicious, life-threatening danger to humanity:

- Always ready to attack
- Lizard-like appearance
- Portrayal in movies: enemy waiting in ambush
- Frightening noises

FACTS

- Very intelligent animal
- Capable of being tamed and trained
- Danger to humans only when provoked
- Rare for a crocodile to attack a human being

PHYSICAL CHARACTERISTICS

- Long body, ranging from six to twenty feet
- Horny plate cover that provides protection from other predators
- Short legs that end in clawed, webbed toes
- Long snout with a very large mouth, razor-sharp, cone-shaped teeth
- Weapons for fighting:
  - Powerful jaws
  - Long, massive tail that can knock an enemy unconscious

BEHAVIOR

- Spends most of its time partly submerged in water
  - Can stay under water for long periods of time
  - Nose, eyes, and ears high up on its head, allowing it to breathe, see, and hear while mostly under water.
- Roars to establish its own territory
- Hisses in warning
- Eats meat—small animals

HABITAT

Found in many parts of the world:

- Tropical climates
- Subtropical climates

15–4. COMPARING AND CONTRASTING THE ESSAY AND THE BULLETED SUMMARY

Directions: Read the two versions of "The Crocodile" found on Sheets 15–1 and 15–3, and then compare and contrast the two versions by answering the questions on this sheet.

1. Place the two formats side by side. Describe what you see when you look at them, even before reading them.

   a. Essay: _____

   _____

   b. Bulleted summary: _____

   _____

2. Briefly describe the beginning of each version.

   a. What is accomplished in the first paragraph of the essay? _____

   _____

   _____

   b. What is accomplished in the initial two lines of the bulleted summary? _____

   _____

   _____

3. Briefly describe the end of each version.

   a. What is accomplished in the last paragraph of the essay? _____

   _____

   _____

   b. What is accomplished in the final lines of the bulleted summary? _____

   _____

   _____

4. Both versions communicate the same information.

   a. Which uses more words? _____

   b. Which takes up more space? _____

15–4. Comparing and Contrasting the Essay and the Bulleted Summary Continued

5. What difference can you see in the words used in the two versions? _____

_____

_____

6. Describe the sentence structure of each version:

   a. Essay: _____

   _____

   b. Bulleted summary: _____

   _____

7. Which format flows more smoothly, and why is it important that it flow more smoothly?

   _____

   _____

   _____

8. If you were interested in the noises made by the crocodile, which version would get you to the information most quickly? How is this version able to let you immediately spot what you want?

   _____

   _____

   _____

9. Both the essay and the bulleted summary are legitimate modes of communication, but each serves a different purpose and is directed at a different reader. What do you suppose was the purpose of each format of the two samples, and to what audience might each be directed?

   a. Essay purpose: _____

   _____

   Essay audience: _____

   _____

   b. Bulleted summary purpose: _____

   _____

   Bulleted summary audience: _____

   _____

15–5. DIFFERENCES BETWEEN THE ESSAY AND THE BULLETED SUMMARY
(answers to Sheet 15–4)

1. a. The essay is presented in traditional paragraphing form.
   b. The bulleted summary presents information under headings and thus is presented in fragmented groupings of words. It also takes presentation into account through the use of listing, underlining, bullets, and white space.

2. a. The essay begins with a formal, introductory paragraph that establishes the purpose or thesis of the communication and attempts to establish interest in (or the authority of) the essay.
   b. The bulleted summary begins with a statement of focus (what the communication is about) and an overview that establishes the most important pieces of information.

3. a. The essay ends with a formal, concluding paragraph that summarizes what the essay has communicated and repeats its main point(s).
   b. The bulleted summary ends with additional information that is pertinent but not essential.

4. a. The traditional essay uses more words because it requires complete sentences as well as words for transitions. It also has an introductory and concluding paragraph that the bulleted summary does not have.
   b. The bulleted summary normally takes more space (especially if it is double spaced) because of concern with the presentation.

5. The words in the essay tend to be more sophisticated and varied than in the bulleted summary, which uses simpler vocabulary.

6. a. The essay requires complete sentences.
   b. The bulleted summary does not require complete sentences; use of fragments (in lists) is acceptable and even encouraged.

7. The essay is the more smoothly flowing format because it is assumed the reader will read it in its entirety. The smoothness assists the reader in completing the task. The reader is more likely to read only parts of the bulleted summary, moving directly to the pertinent information and skipping over the rest.

8. The bulleted summary would get you to the information more quickly because you would be able to use the headings to guide you to the information you want. "Behavior" leads you to information about crocodile noises.

9. The essay is often used in the academic world to communicate with instructors, to convince them of your understanding of topics or the validity of your analyses. It is also a common form in some publications (magazine columns, opinion pieces in newspapers), usually to persuade or entertain readers. It is assumed the reader will read the entire essay, which is expected to project a sense of the author's style.

   The bulleted summary is used to communicate information as clearly and succinctly as possible. It is assumed that people seeking specific information will skip over information they do not need. The bulleted summary seeks to make information accessible for easy reference. It makes few assumptions about readers' interests and minimizes style.

Session 16. WRITING A BULLETED SUMMARY

In this session, students create a bulleted summary from someone else's essay.

OBJECTIVE

The students will translate an essay into a bulleted summary, making the material more concise.

PROCEDURE

1. Hand out Sheet 16–1, "Create a Bulleted Summary," and Sheet 16–2, "Your Friend's Essay." Discuss the scenario on the sheets, which is also outlined in the "Setting the Stage" section of Session 15.
2. Tell the class to rewrite the essay as a bulleted summary following the directions on Sheet 16–1.
3. Collect and grade the bulleted summaries. Project on a screen or reproduce and hand out summaries from the class as well as a copy of the sample answer below. Discuss the merits of the bulleted summaries students submitted.

POSSIBLE ANSWER

SUGGESTIONS FOR YOUR INTERN PROGRAM

Based on my experiences as an intern this summer, I have three recommendations for your intern program. I believe they will make the experiences of future interns as rewarding as mine and make your interns as valuable as possible for you.

1. *Introduce your new intern to many people.*

   Before the summer ended, I worked with nearly everyone in the company. Knowing who the people were helped me get

   • The right help
   • The right information

   My boss didn't need to tell me whom to see for help; I already knew.

2. *Explain what is expected of the intern.*
   My boss helped me become self-sufficient because she

   • Gave me specific jobs to do
   • Taught me what was expected from each job
   • Told me what jobs must be performed each week

3. *Invite the intern in early.*
   Inviting me in the week before starting work gave me

   • An overview of the company and job
   • A week to sort through my experiences

   The result was that I felt very comfortable on the job right away.

Name _____ Date _____

16–1. CREATE A BULLETED SUMMARY

Directions: Your friend has just spent the summer working as an intern. A vice president of the company has asked her to write recommendations for the intern program based on her own successful experiences. Your friend has written the essay on Sheet 16–2. After reviewing it, you suggest that a bulleted summary would reflect better on your friend. You offer to create a bulleted summary from your friend's essay. She accepts. After reading your friend's essay on Sheet 16–2, follow the directions below to create a bulleted summary from her essay.

1. Read through your friend's essay completely.

2. Locate three sentences that define your friend's suggestions for the intern program. Create a heading for each suggestion, something that defines the idea at a glance. Number and underline the headings to make them easier to scan.

3. Support each heading with material you find in the essay. Use only the material you consider necessary to explain each of your friend's ideas.

4. Write an overview for your summary. Make the overview friendly, but get right to the point of introducing the material. Can you use any of the remaining essay material in your overview?

5. Look for ways to use visual elements: white space, lists, boldface, etc.

6. Create a title. When you are finished, turn your work in to your teacher.

16–2. YOUR FRIEND'S ESSAY

Here is the essay your friend wrote at the request of one of the company's vice presidents. See Sheet 16–1, "Create a Bulleted Summary," for instructions for rewriting it as a bulleted summary.

Working as an intern this summer has taught me valuable lessons about the world of business. Reflecting on my experiences, I have discovered that they may prove valuable to you, too, and the future of your intern program.

Meeting nearly everyone when I first arrived excited me. Your company employs many interesting people. The number of jobs in your company surprised me. But I realized that meeting people early had a purpose beyond just being friendly.

Before the summer ended, I worked with nearly everyone. True, I worked with some people only once; others, three or four times. But knowing who people were helped me get the right help and information when I needed it.

As a result of knowing people, I found myself capable of acting on orders from my boss. She told me to get some information. She didn't need to tell me who to see. I knew who to see. She liked that. She said she appreciated my help because I actually helped and didn't nag her. You might consider introducing future interns to many people early.

I would have nagged my boss, but she really helped me to become self-sufficient. I was handling jobs myself without help from anyone when I left. But that wasn't all my own doing. When I started, my boss gave me a list of specific jobs. She taught me what she wanted me to do for each one. She also told me that the jobs had to be performed every week. Though special jobs arose during the summer, I knew I had those responsibilities every week. My boss taking that time to help me get started really helped. For the future of your intern program, you might consider giving interns specific assignments when they first start.

My boss helped me in another way. A week before I started, she invited me to come in for two hours. That really helped. I felt overwhelmed by all that was new in those two hours. But during the next week at home, I had a chance to sort through my experiences. When I started, I felt comfortable. You might also consider inviting your new intern in a week early.

My boss really made a difference. If the boss for your new intern is like her, they'll find the experience as rewarding and enjoyable as mine was.

Session 17. MIXING FORMATS

One aim of writing is to make information accessible. Sometimes that means mixing elements of different formats. Thus, writers might use elements from both the essay and bulleted summary in a single work.

In this session, students revise an earlier essay to make their ideas more accessible. This exercise works well on a word processor (particularly if the original essays are available on disk).

OBJECTIVE

The students will revise an essay using elements of the bulleted summary format.

SETTING THE STAGE

Often, the best way to present information economically is not by choosing between the essay and bulleted summary, but by combining the two:

- The essay can persuade and give a sense of the author's style.
- The bulleted summary can eliminate unnecessary words and help the reader grasp supporting material quickly.

For example, in an essay, a writer may bullet two or more key paragraphs to draw attention to important information. Or the writer might add headings to an essay to emphasize organization. (The opening paragraph of this "Setting the Stage" section combines elements of both formats.)

Once the student realizes that elements of the different formats can be combined, many new ways to present information open.

PROCEDURE

1. Hand out the essays students wrote in Session 7 (trying to persuade someone to be more concise) or another recent set of essays suitable for this assignment. Persuasive essays tend to work best.
2. On the board, write the following:

   Rewrite your persuasive essay, using elements from the bulleted summary format. Consider using bulleted lists, white space, headings, and other visual elements. Remember, though, that you are trying to persuade someone to change, so you cannot merely make facts accessible.

Section 3

Organizing and Revising Work

ORGANIZING AND REVISING WORK

At work, John Guzman hates to receive papers from Yvonne Quinn. Yvonne is a wonderful writer. She possesses excellent control of the language, and she writes concisely. But she is not writing to meet John's needs. He has to work to dig out the information he wants.

Today, many of the best writers we produce are like Yvonne. They lack skills to organize materials for different audiences. The perfect piece for one audience may bury vital information for another. From the writer's perspective, revising for a different audience is a tedious chore—one that the writer, more often than not, would rather not be bothered with. As a result, communication suffers or fails completely.

This section presents a technique called *cutting and pasting* that takes the pain out of revising. It gives writers a quick, efficient way to manipulate blocks of information. The technique opens possibilities for students to experiment with organizing information in many ways to decide what is best for an audience.

Section Three contains nine sessions. If word processing equipment is available, it can be used in all nine sessions. Just enter and store the exercise sheets on disk. Once students know the commands for defining and moving blocks, paragraphs, or sentences, cutting and pasting works very well on a word processor.

Session 18. Cutting and Pasting Blocks of Ideas

Revising is a creative act, but the labor of writing the revision can be tedious, time consuming, and boring. Most students do not like to revise their work— *although revising is essential for producing concise, effective communication.* This exercise teaches students a cutting and pasting technique that takes a lot of the pain out of revising.

Session 19. Cutting and Pasting to Add and Delete Ideas

In this session, students take the next step in the cutting and pasting approach. They add new ideas and delete unnecessary material.

Session 20. Cutting and Pasting Ideas Alphanumerically

In this session, students work with the first of four models to help organize material. This exercise asks them to reorganize material into alphabetical and numerical order.

Session 21. Cutting and Pasting Ideas into Time Sequence

In this exercise, students reorganize material into chronological order.

Session 22. Cutting and Pasting Ideas by Categories

Students use the same material as in Session 21, this time organizing it by categories rather than by chronology.

Session 23. Cutting and Pasting into Order of Importance

In this session, students work with a fourth model for organizing information, by establishing priorities for the audience. This may be the most difficult way to order material, but it is a commonly used organizational pattern.

Session 24. What's the Best Order?

Students have been experimenting with different ways to organize information. In this session, they will decide for different situations which of the four patterns they have learned works best.

Session 25. Cutting and Pasting Individual Work into a Team Paper

Students produce a team paper by cutting and pasting together elements from individuals' work. This session helps students evaluate material, choose among alternatives, and develop negotiating skills. It also helps students focus on the language used to express an idea.

Session 26. Polishing the Team's Work

Polishing a team's work is an excellent exercise in the discipline of writing. Individuals must refrain from reinserting their own ideas and biases to be fair to the group. They must also learn to contribute to the work of the whole and to accept compromise. In this session, each student revises the team's consolidated work from Session 25.

Session 18. CUTTING AND PASTING BLOCKS OF IDEAS

Revising is a creative act, but the labor of writing the revision is tedious and time consuming. Most students do not like to revise their work— although revising is essential to producing concise, effective communication. This exercise teaches students a cutting and pasting technique that takes a lot of the pain out of revising.

OBJECTIVES

The students will

- Analyze an essay to determine a logical sequence of presentation
- Identify common organizational patterns for essays
- Revise an essay by cutting and pasting paragraphs into a logical sequence

SETTING THE STAGE

Rarely does a first draft convey information concisely. Typically, concise writing requires a second, third, or even fourth draft. Repeatedly copying over much of the same information, however, is boring and takes time that could be better focused on the revising process itself. Also, every time material is rewritten, new mistakes can crop up—or valuable material can be overlooked.

A simple technique called cutting and pasting helps overcome these problems. As the name implies, you cut a work into parts, reorganize the parts on a clean sheet of paper, and paste or tape them down when you are happy with the new organization.

Most word processing programs have commands that allow cutting and pasting on the screen (common terms are MOVE and BLOCK), but you do not need access to a word processor to benefit from this technique. You can cut and paste with scissors and tape.

PROCEDURE

1. If your students do this exercise in class, you will need to provide scissors, tape, and blank paper for them, in addition to copies of Sheets 18–1 and 18–2.

2. Discuss with students the importance of revising work and review the actual process of revising they currently use. Ask them to describe the actual steps they take when they revise.

3. Hand out Sheet 18–1, "How to Cut and Paste," and Sheet 18–2, "Paragraphs to Cut and Paste." Explain how cutting and pasting works and review organization patterns as discussed on Sheet 18–1.

4. Remind students to

   • Leave the letter tags on the paragraphs when they paste them down

   • Write their names at the top of the new paper

   • Write the letter order of the paragraphs and type of organizational pattern they followed at the bottom

ANSWERS

There are a number of reasonable possibilities. The most common organizational pattern will be chronological, with a paragraph letter sequence of C, E, B, D, F, A.

18–1. HOW TO CUT AND PASTE

INFORMATION

Cutting and pasting can make revising your work easier by eliminating the need to copy the whole piece over repeatedly.

Using a pair of scissors, you cut out blocks of ideas from your work so you can rearrange them. When you are happy with the new order, you paste, or tape, the paragraphs onto a clean sheet of paper. Only when you are happy with the overall order do you recopy the whole work.

You can apply this technique at many levels. You can cut and paste

- Blocks or paragraphs
- Sentences within a paragraph
- Lists
- Headings or subheadings

You can also cut open a paragraph and insert new ideas within it, or add transitional sentences between paragraphs.

ORGANIZATIONAL PATTERNS

Here are some of the most common organizational patterns used in essays:

- Order of importance (most to least or least to most)
- Chronological (time order)
- Cause and effect
- General to specific (or specific to general)
- Problem/solution
- Comparison and contrast

DIRECTIONS

On Sheet 18–2 you will find six paragraphs about soccer, lettered A through F. Your assignment is to cut them apart and reorganize them into a logical presentation order. Assume that your audience is a high school soccer team, and your purpose is to enrich their experience as players of the game.

1. Cut each paragraph along the dotted lines. Make sure you include the identification letter.
2. Rearrange the paragraphs to your satisfaction; then paste (or tape) them down on a blank piece of paper.
3. Write your name at the top of the new paper.
4. At the bottom of the paper with the paragraphs pasted on it, write the letter order you used and the organizational pattern you followed (see above for examples).

18–2. PARAGRAPHS FOR CUTTING AND PASTING

See Directions on Sheet 18–1, "How to Cut and Paste."

A.   Over the years the violence began to decrease as rules began to emerge. At first each team tried to establish its own rules, but as more schools became involved, consistent regulations evolved. "Association football" or soccer, as we know it, grew in popularity around the world while American football began to receive the attention of the United States.

B.   The Ancient Romans' version of soccer was "harpastium," a game which used a ball that was the inflated bladder of an animal. The ball was kicked, thrown, carried, or batted toward a goal, and participants were often injured because there were no rules about hurting an opponent.

C.   One of the most popular sports around the world is a game known as football in most countries but as soccer in the United States. Soccer is a fast-paced sport that often ignites the emotions of spectators. This should not surprise anyone who knows the history of the sport, because it is wrought with violence.

D.   During the Middle Ages, a game similar to Roman soccer was found in Italy. It was a game that involved hundreds of players, often whole towns playing against each other. The goals were commonly in the separate towns, miles apart. The games were called "melees" and were very dangerous to the participants.

E.   Soccer as we know it can probably be traced to China in about 3 B.C. and a game the Chinese enjoyed called "tsu chu." The players ran after a ball of leather and were allowed to attack each other as well as the ball. The game was usually played before the emperor, and the winners received rich gifts. The losers were often whipped.

F.   As the years went on, the game became more and more violent. In the British empire, "football" became exceptionally perilous to the participants. For example, in Scotland, teams of married women competed against single women. The winners often beat up the losers. In England, the game began to gain popularity with school children, but they copied the way adults played, including punching, kicking, and butting. In 1365, King Edward II tried to ban the game, but the ban was all but ignored.

Session 19. CUTTING AND PASTING TO ADD AND DELETE IDEAS

In this session, students take the next step in revising. They use cutting and pasting to add new ideas and delete unnecessary material.

OBJECTIVES

The students will

- Sequence information
- Edit by introducing new ideas into a sequence
- Edit by eliminating unnecessary information

SETTING THE STAGE

Revising requires more than moving information around. As you move ideas to establish new relationships, new ideas often emerge. Sometimes you discover that information is missing, or that you can eliminate some material because it is redundant or irrelevant.

However, when students revise using a draft that is frozen on paper, they often hesitate to add or delete because it will mean copying over the draft an extra time. Cutting and pasting can make adding and deleting easier.

PROCEDURE

1. If the exercise is to be done in class, make sure you have scissors and tape for each student.

2. Review with the class the need to check a completed draft to make certain that all material is relevant to the purpose of the writing and that sufficient detail is provided to be clear and/or convincing.

3. Hand out Sheet 19–1, "Revising *How to Change a Tire.*" Tell students that an expert has jotted down notes for new drivers on how to change tires. The students need to rearrange these notes so a new driver has logical, step-by-step instructions for changing a tire. Remind the students to tape each paragraph with a single piece of tape along the side so the paragraph can be moved again.

4. Once the notes have been rearranged, ask students to try to identify additional information the reader might need to complete the task. Students should be careful not to make too many assumptions about what background the reader has for changing tires. Have the students write additional information on separate paper that they will then cut and insert (paste) into the instructions.

5. Once ideas are complete, students should cross out as many unnecessary or irrelevant ideas as possible. They can then turn in their cut-and-pasted work without recopying it.

6. If you grade the work, we recommend the following emphases:

   • 50 percent for organization
   • 40 percent for new ideas
   • 10 percent for editing

ANSWER

One solution would organize the paragraphs in the order A, F, D, C, B, E. Suggestions for additions and deletions are included in brackets [ ] in the sample solution below. Note that not all new ideas require new paragraphs. They can be added at the beginning, end, or middle of existing paragraphs.

A. When you get a flat tire, you should follow these instructions. [delete: It is frustrating to get a flat tire, but you must deal with it.]

F. [delete: It is very important to remember that when] [add: Once] you have a flat tire, [delete: you should] get off the road as quickly and safely as possible. Drive to a shoulder on the side of the road or take the next exit if there is no shoulder. Make sure you're out of traffic and that no on-coming traffic can hit you. [new idea: If possible, set up flares or reflectors or have someone signal traffic to warn drivers to avoid your car.] [new idea: If you or your parents belong to AAA or another motor club, call them to come out and fix your flat. If you don't belong to a club, you will need to change your tire yourself.]

D. Check to see if you have a spare tire and if it has air. If the spare doesn't have air, don't bother changing it. [new idea: Walk to the nearest gas station and ask for help.] [new idea: You ought to check that you have all the equipment you need before you get started. You should have a jack and a jack bar. You should also have a block of wood, but it's not absolutely necessary.]

C. If you have all the necessary equipment, place the jack under the car near the flat tire. [delete: The second thing you should do is this:] If you have a block of wood, place it in front of a tire with air so the car won't move.

B. If you have a hubcap, remove it. [new idea: by prying the flat end of the jack bar under its edge.] Now loosen, but don't remove, the lug nuts [delete: . You don't need a wrench. You can use] with the jack bar for this purpose also.

E. Raise the car, and once the tire is off the ground, finish removing the lug nuts. Once the tire is unbolted, lift it off. Put the new tire on and attach it by putting the lug nuts back on, tightening them by hand. Using the jack, lower the car and then securely tighten the lug nuts using the jack bar. [new ideas: Replace the hubcap. Put away the flat tire, the jack, the jack bar, and the block of wood. You're ready to drive off.]

Name _____ Date _____

19-1. REVISING *HOW TO CHANGE A TIRE*

Directions: You are preparing instructions for a new driver on how to change a flat tire on a car. You have received some notes from an expert, but he or she may not have thought of everything.

1. Reorganize the instructions into logical order by pasting them onto a sheet of blank paper. Tape each paragraph temporarily with a single piece of tape on the side. Leave space between paragraphs so you can add ideas.
2. Read through the new draft. Does it make sense? If it doesn't, move the paragraphs.
3. Are any important steps or ideas missing? If so, write them on another sheet of paper; then neatly cut them out. Now paste them into the instructions where appropriate. *Note*: You may cut a paragraph apart to provide space to paste in a new idea.
4. Cross out words, phrases, or sentences that are not necessary.
5. Write your name on the revised essay and hand it in.

A.   When you get a flat tire, you should follow these instructions. It is frustrating to get a flat tire, but you must deal with it.

B.   If you have a hubcap, remove it. Now loosen, but don't remove, the lug nuts. You don't need a wrench. You can use the jack bar for this purpose also.

C.   If you have all the necessary equipment, place the jack under the car near the flat tire. The second thing you should do is this: If you have a block of wood, place it in front of a tire with air so the car won't move.

D.   Check to see if you have a spare tire and if it has air. If the spare doesn't have air, don't bother changing it.

E.   Raise the car, and once the tire is off the ground, finish removing the lug nuts. Once the tire is unbolted, lift it off. Put the new tire on and attach it by putting the lug nuts back on, tightening them by hand. Using the jack, lower the car and then securely tighten the lug nuts using the jack bar.

F.   It is very important to remember that when you have a flat tire, you should get off the road as quickly and safely as possible. Drive to a shoulder on the side of the road or take the next exit if there is no shoulder. Make sure you're out of traffic and that no on-coming traffic can hit you.

Session 20. CUTTING AND PASTING IDEAS ALPHANUMERICALLY

In this session, students work with the first of four models to help organize material. The exercise asks them to reorganize material into alphanumerical order.

OBJECTIVES

The students will

- Analyze information for alphabetical/numerical relationships
- Reorganize material based on alphabetical/numerical relationships

SETTING THE STAGE

A telephone book offers a convenient way to find someone's phone number. If you know someone's last name, you simply look up the listing. What makes it so simple is the alphabetical organization of the data.

Random bits of information mean nothing. You would be hard pressed to find someone's telephone number if the names and numbers were jumbled together randomly. Putting the pieces of data in order adds value and meaning, but it has to be the right order for the purpose. The telephone book could be organized numerically by phone number, but that wouldn't help you call someone.

Alphabetical and numerical (often shortened as alphanumeric) order is a familiar way to organize data. We all know how to organize information alphabetically by first letter (or the second letter, when two words have the same first letter, etc.). Numbers can be arranged in ascending order (1, 2, 3) or descending order (3, 2, 1). For instance, you might use ascending order for the winners of a contest and descending order for a list of cars with the best gas mileage. You can also organize by letters *and* numbers, such as A1, A2, A3, B1, B2, C1, C2; or 1A, 1B, 1C, 2A, 2B, etc.

PROCEDURE

1. Discuss with your students how to organize material alphanumerically.
2. Hand out Sheet 20–1, "Organizing Material Alphabetically," and Sheet 20–2, "Organizing Material Numerically." Students should

use the cut and paste technique to reorganize the entries on a blank piece of paper.

3. Remind students to include the following information on the reorganized sheets they hand in:

- Their name at the top
- The letter order of the paragraphs at the bottom
- The organizational pattern they followed (alphabetical or numerical)

ANSWERS

The sequence for alphabetical order is E, D, A, C, F, G, B, H. The sequence for numerical order is D, C, F, H, E, A, G, B.

Name _____   Date _____

20-1. ORGANIZING MATERIAL ALPHABETICALLY

Directions: Two elementary schools, Forrest and Comstone, held a competition to encourage reading. Each class recorded the number of books students read for pleasure for six weeks. The results are listed below in random order. Each time a question arises, the contest judges must look through the entire list to find a teacher's record. You have been asked to make it easier to find teacher information by organizing the records alphabetically by teachers' last names. Cut out and reorganize the records on a sheet of blank paper. IMPORTANT: On the reorganized list, write your name at the top and the letter order of your records at the bottom. Also write the organizational pattern (alphabetical).

A. Agnes Fazio   Forrest Academy   Room 106

This class read a total of 178 books. Last year they read only 125. Mrs. Fazio has been with the school three years.

B. Samantha McCain   Forrest Academy   Room 109

Everyone in class read at least ten books. They read 155 as a class. Ms. McCain is a first year teacher.

C. Margo Hernandez   Forrest Academy   Room 112

This class read 198 books. Mrs. Hernandez's classes have come in first in three contests in the last five years.

D. Norman Davies   Forrest Academy   Room 104

This class read 201 books. Mr. Davies has taught at Forrest for eight years and has directed the school play the last three years.

E. Bettylynne Beren   Comstone Elementary   Room 4C

This class read 181 books. Mrs. Beren arrived at Comstone last year; she won five teaching awards in her previous schools in Arizona.

F. Michael Katz   Comstone Elementary   Room 4D

Mr. Katz encouraged his class to read 193 books. He has taught for ten years.

G. Jessica Lally   Comstone Elementary   Room 5E

The class read 176 books, though it has the smallest number of students in the contest. Ms. Lally serves on the Literacy Committee.

H. Dana Sherman   Forrest Academy   Room 102

The class read a total of 183 books. Mr. Sherman's class has won the contest once before.

20–2. ORGANIZING MATERIAL NUMERICALLY

Directions: Who won the contest? Who came in second? Last? Organize the records numerically by the number of books read. Use the cut and paste technique to reorganize the records on a sheet of blank paper. IMPORTANT: Write your name at the top and the letter order of your records at the bottom of the reorganized list. Also write the organizational pattern (numerical).

A. Agnes Fazio   Forrest Academy   Room 106

This class read a total of 178 books. Last year they read only 125. Mrs. Fazio has been with the school three years.

B. Samantha McCain   Forrest Academy   Room 109

Everyone in class read at least ten books. They read 155 as a class. Ms. McCain is a first year teacher.

C. Margo Hernandez   Forrest Academy   Room 112

This class read 198 books. Mrs. Hernandez's classes have come in first in three contests in the last five years.

D. Norman Davies   Forrest Academy   Room 104

This class read 201 books. Mr. Davies has taught at Forrest for eight years and has directed the school play the last three years.

E. Bettylynne Beren   Comstone Elementary   Room 4C

This class read 181 books. Mrs. Beren arrived at Comstone last year; she won five teaching awards in her previous schools in Arizona.

F. Michael Katz   Comstone Elementary   Room 4D

Mr. Katz encouraged his class to read 193 books. He has taught for ten years.

G. Jessica Lally   Comstone Elementary   Room 5E

The class read 176 books, though it has the smallest number of students in the contest. Ms. Lally serves on the Literacy Committee.

H. Dana Sherman   Forrest Academy   Room 102

The class read a total of 183 books. Mr. Sherman's class has won the contest once before.

Session 21. CUTTING AND PASTING IDEAS INTO TIME SEQUENCE

In this exercise, students reorganize material into chronological order.

OBJECTIVES

The students will

- Analyze information for time relationships
- Reorganize material based on chronology

SETTING THE STAGE

One common way to organize ideas and information is into time sequence, or chronological order. You can organize material chronologically beginning with what happened first and ending with what happened last, or you can reverse that order.

You may want to discuss with the class when they would use chronological order. It is an ideal organizational pattern for

- Instructions and directions
- Historical lists and reviews
- Explanations ("What happened?")
- Legal cases

See if the class can add to the list.

PROCEDURE

1. If this is to be done in class, you will need scissors, tape, and two sheets of blank paper for each student.
2. Hand out Sheet 21–1, "Organizing Ideas into Time Sequence." It features paragraphs for an essay about how the family has changed. The objective is to organize the essay for a history class that is studying families through the ages.
3. Tell students to cut apart the essays and paste them into chronological order. Remind them to write their names on the reorganized essays and the letter order of the paragraphs on the bottom, along with the organizational pattern (chronological).

4. If you taught about the bulleted summary from Section Two, you may want to have the students review that format while revising this material.

ANSWERS

The letter sequence of paragraphs should be A, E, F, G, H, I, J, K, L, B, C, D, M.

21-1. ORGANIZING IDEAS INTO TIME SEQUENCE

Directions: The following paragraphs contain material that will be used for an essay on the family. Your audience is a high school history class beginning to study families. Your objective is to provide facts. Read through the material. Using cut and paste techniques, rearrange the material in strict chronological order on two separate sheets of paper. IMPORTANT: Write your name at the top and the letter order of your rearranged paragraphs at the bottom of the revised essay.

A.   What is a family?

B.   During this century, the "typical" family has changed dramatically in America. In 1900, the average family still lived on a farm, supporting many children who helped with the chores. This was an extended family because relatives often lived near each other and sometimes in the same home. It was common for grandparents to live with their children's families. Sometimes brothers and sisters clustered together in the same home with their children. Children usually worked long days, as long as adults, and few were educated beyond basic skills.

C.   By the 1950s, the "nuclear" family was the norm: father, mother, and children, living apart from other family members. Grandparents and uncles and aunts, with their children, were out of the picture because they often lived some distance away. The lives of children, however, had improved. Labor laws prohibited most young children from working long hours. Medical research was wiping out many childhood diseases.

D.   By the 1980s, the family unit looked complex. Nearly a majority of families were led by divorced parents. Often, divorced parents married each other, creating "blended" families with children from different marriages. A large number of families were also headed by single parents, many of these by single women. Kids had become a consumer force in their own right. New laws sought to protect them from abuse not only in the workplace but at home.

E.   The family itself has changed throughout history.

F.   Early humans organized communities along family lines. Extended families, or clans, lived together.

G. In Ancient China, so little value was placed on daughters that a father, when asked how many children he had, would only raise fingers for his sons.

H. In Medieval Europe, children were seen simply as small adults—and treated as such. Plagues, war, and famine transfigured families. Parents and children died, and survivors banded together to create "blended families."

I. In the early 1600s in England, unmarried mothers and abandoned children became serious problems. Communities enacted laws that prohibited these families from moving into town because this would require raising taxes for supporting them.

J. Some of these families emigrated from England to America in the early 1600s, where they created new blended families. By coming to America, others severed family ties. They searched for new family relationships. One elderly man, for example, hired a son to care for him in his old age.

K. Civil wars raged in Japan in the early 1600s. In one area, family life was held in such low esteem that infanticide was common. By the mid-1600s, strong leadership emerged that set the stage for peace for two centuries. Families flourished. Parents highly regarded and indulged their children. Daughters were schooled and valued.

L. In the late 1800s new ideas about family emerged. According to communist theory, children belonged not to their parents, but to the state. Children's first allegiance should be to the state, not their parents. Fascist dictatorships adopted these ideas in the twentieth century. The Soviet Union, Hitler's Germany, Mussolini's Italy, and communist China all experimented with these new notions of family.

M. Families are different today from those of fifty years ago. They, in turn, were different from the models of a century ago. It is certain that tomorrow the typical family will change once again.

Session 22. CUTTING AND PASTING IDEAS BY CATEGORIES

Students use the same paragraphs as in Session 21, but this time they organize the material by categories, not by time.

OBJECTIVES

The students will

- Create categories for grouping information
- Analyze material with categories in mind
- Organize material by category

SETTING THE STAGE

Another way to organize information is to create categories for grouping common material. For example, a telephone book has already categorized numbers by calling area. Within that broad category, it lists names alphabetically. A guidebook to a large city might categorize information by

- Restaurants
- Hotels
- Museums
- Shops
- Points of interest
- Tours

Or, the guidebook could present the same information categorized by areas of the city. In this case, the authors assume the readers want to know what is nearby as they walk through an area. Note that once information is sorted by category, it can then be organized within each category, perhaps by one of the following patterns:

- Chronological
- Alphabetical or numerical
- Other categories (such as price range)

The reader's needs should determine the right categories for presenting information. The writer must analyze what categories would best help the reader make use of the information to be presented.

Often, categorizing information reveals that important information is missing. In this exercise students will also look for areas where information is incomplete.

PROCEDURE

1. If students are going to be doing the work in class, have scissors, tape, and two pieces of blank paper for each of them.

2. Discuss the organization of material in categories, using the information in "Setting the Stage" above.

3. Hand out Sheet 22–1, "Organizing by Category." (Note that although it contains the same material as Sheet 21–1, it does not carry letter labels for each paragraph. This is because students will be doing more than just rearranging existing information and because there is no one correct order for the paragraphs.)

4. Explain to students that they will be drawing from the material on Sheet 22–1 to help a United States ambassador prepare for a meeting on the family with representatives from Great Britain, the People's Republic of China, Russia, and Italy. The ambassador wants background on families in these countries. You will use the material as the first source to prepare a briefing paper.

5. Discuss with the class different ways to organize the material. The discussion should quickly converge on creating categories for each country. How should the categories be ordered? One way is alphabetically by country name; another possibility is by geographical region (so that, for instance, Japan and China are together).

6. Tell students to cut apart and arrange paragraphs into the categories decided on, leaving room to write in appropriate headings. They should try to provide the same kind of information for each category.

7. Discuss why the sheet recommends that students organize material within categories from most recent to most ancient. What would be most relevant to the ambassador?

8. Ask students to review their organized material, paying particular attention to information missing from some of the categories. For instance, family life in the United States today is covered, but what about the other countries? Material remains to be found for them. Students should indicate what material is still needed by writing notes in the margins next to where the material would be inserted.

9. This is a good candidate for rewriting as a bulleted summary, if you want to review that format.

ANSWERS

Students' papers will vary. Collect the fully reorganized essays and grade for organization and missing material indicated.

Name _____   Date _____

22-1. ORGANIZING IDEAS INTO TIME SEQUENCE

Directions: Using the cutting and pasting technique, prepare a briefing paper for a busy ambassador from the material provided. Organize according to categories your class decided will help the ambassador meet the delegates to a conference on the family. Paste your material under appropriate category headings, with most recent information first and oldest information last. Then review your revised piece and write notes in the margins about any information you would still need to locate if you were to complete this briefing paper. IMPORTANT: Write your name at the top of the revised piece.

What is a family?

During this century, the "typical" family has changed dramatically in America. In 1900, the average family still lived on a farm, supporting many children who helped with the chores. This was an extended family because relatives often lived near each other and sometimes in the same home. It was common for grandparents to live with their children's families. Sometimes brothers and sisters clustered together in the same home with their children. Children usually worked long days, as long as adults, and few were educated beyond basic skills.

By the 1950s, the "nuclear" family was the norm: father, mother, and children, living apart from other family members. Grandparents and uncles and aunts, with their children, were out of the picture because they often lived some distance away. The lives of children, however, had improved. Labor laws prohibited most young children from working long hours. Medical research was wiping out many childhood diseases.

By the 1980s, the family unit looked complex. Nearly a majority of families were led by divorced parents. Often, divorced parents married each other, creating "blended" families with children from different marriages. A large number of families were also headed by single parents, many of these by single women. Kids had become a consumer force in their own right. New laws sought to protect them from abuse not only in the workplace but at home.

The family itself has changed throughout history.

Early humans organized communities along family lines. Extended families, or clans, lived together.

22–1. *Organizing Ideas Into Time Sequence Continued*

In Ancient China, so little value was placed on daughters that a father, when asked how many children he had, would only raise fingers for his sons.

In Medieval Europe, children were seen simply as small adults—and treated as such. Plagues, war, and famine transfigured families. Parents and children died, and survivors banded together to create "blended families."

In the early 1600s in England, unmarried mothers and abandoned children became serious problems. Communities enacted laws that prohibited these families from moving into town because this would require raising taxes for supporting them.

Some of these families emigrated from England to America in the early 1600s, where they created new blended families. By coming to America, others severed family ties. They searched for new family relationships. One elderly man, for example, hired a son to care for him in his old age.

Civil wars raged in Japan in the early 1600s. In one area, family life was held in such low esteem that infanticide was common. By the mid-1600s, strong leadership emerged that set the stage for peace for two centuries. Families flourished. Parents highly regarded and indulged their children. Daughters were schooled and valued.

In the late 1800s new ideas about family emerged. According to communist theory, children belonged not to their parents, but to the state. Children's first allegiance should be to the state, not their parents. Fascist dictatorships adopted these ideas in the twentieth century. The Soviet Union, Hitler's Germany, Mussolini's Italy, and communist China all experimented with these new notions of family.

Families are different today from those of fifty years ago. They, in turn, were different from the models of a century ago. It is certain that tomorrow the typical family will change once again.

Session 23. CUTTING AND PASTING INTO ORDER OF IMPORTANCE

In this session, students work with a fourth model of organizing information: establishing priorities for the audience and ordering information accordingly. This may be the most difficult way to organize material, but it is a technique often used today.

OBJECTIVES

The students will

- Analyze information to create categories
- Distinguish more important from less important information
- Establish a priority ranking for material

SETTING THE STAGE

In presenting information, you often need to make decisions for your audience about what is important for them to read. You cannot always rely on them to make their way through an alphanumerical, chronological, or categorical arrangement to find material that is valuable to them. They are busy and have many demands on their time. However, you can try to ensure that they read the most important material by putting it up front. Less valuable information comes later—where it may never be seen.

At first, establishing a priority ranking for information may seem difficult. The writer must distinguish between more important and less important information for a particular audience. There is some guess work involved, but the audience will appreciate the effort even when the priorities are not exactly right.

PROCEDURE

1. Hand out Sheet 23–1, "Organizing Material into Order of Importance," which again presents the paragraphs on the family. This time, students use it to prepare an essay to keep parents alert to dangers children face as a group.
2. Discuss possible ways to categorize information for this new objective.

3. After students reread the material from this new perspective, have them mark and cut out information pertinent to the objective. They may just need sentences from paragraphs.

4. Tell students to organize the clipped material on Sheet 23–2, "Reorganize Your Information," beginning with the most important information to this audience and moving to the least important. They should move information around until they are happy with the order, and then paste it down.

5. On a new sheet of paper and working from the reorganized information, students should write an essay (or a bulleted summary, if you have taught that format) about the dangers that may lie ahead for children. Remind them to concentrate on organizing the material for a busy person.

6. Ask students to hand in both the final essay (or summary) and Sheet 23–2 with the reorganized clips taped to it.

Name _____   Date _____

23–1. ORGANIZING IDEAS INTO ORDER OF IMPORTANCE

Directions: Your audience is a parents group. Your objective is to convince them that while American kids are fairly well off today, that could change, based on what has happened in the past. Reread the paragraphs provided, looking for material you could use to make your case. Make appropriate material (just sentences, in some cases) and cut it out for reorganizing onto Sheet 23–2.

What is a family?

During this century, the "typical" family has changed dramatically in America. In 1900, the average family still lived on a farm, supporting many children who helped with the chores. This was an extended family because relatives often lived near each other and sometimes in the same home. It was common for grandparents to live with their children's families. Sometimes brothers and sisters clustered together in the same home with their children. Children usually worked long days, as long as adults, and few were educated beyond basic skills.

By the 1950s, the "nuclear" family was the norm: father, mother, and children, living apart from other family members. Grandparents and uncles and aunts, with their children, were out of the picture because they often lived some distance away. The lives of children, however, had improved. Labor laws prohibited most young children from working long hours. Medical research was wiping out many childhood diseases.

By the 1980s, the family unit looked complex. Nearly a majority of families were led by divorced parents. Often, divorced parents married each other, creating "blended" families with children from different marriages. A large number of families were also headed by single parents, many of these by single women. Kids had become a consumer force in their own right. New laws sought to protect them from abuse not only in the workplace but at home.

The family itself has changed throughout history.

Early humans organized communities along family lines. Extended families, or clans, lived together.

© 1992 by The Center for Applied Research in Education

In Ancient China, so little value was placed on daughters that a father, when asked how many children he had, would only raise fingers for his sons.

In Medieval Europe, children were seen simply as small adults—and treated as such. Plagues, war, and famine transfigured families. Parents and children died, and survivors banded together to create "blended families."

In the early 1600s in England, unmarried mothers and abandoned children became serious problems. Communities enacted laws that prohibited these families from moving into town because this would require raising taxes for supporting them.

Some of these families emigrated from England to America in the early 1600s, where they created new blended families. By coming to America, others severed family ties. They searched for new family relationships. One elderly man, for example, hired a son to care for him in his old age.

Civil wars raged in Japan in the early 1600s. In one area, family life was held in such low esteem that infanticide was common. By the mid-1600s, strong leadership emerged that set the stage for peace for two centuries. Families flourished. Parents highly regarded and indulged their children. Daughters were schooled and valued.

In the late 1800s new ideas about family emerged. According to communist theory, children belonged not to their parents, but to the state. Children's first allegiance should be to the state, not their parents. Fascist dictatorships adopted these ideas in the twentieth century. The Soviet Union, Hitler's Germany, Mussolini's Italy, and communist China all experimented with these new notions of family.

Families are different today from those of fifty years ago. They, in turn, were different from the models of a century ago. It is certain that tomorrow the typical family will change once again.

Name _____   Date _____

23-2. REORGANIZE YOUR INFORMATION

Directions: On this sheet, arrange information you clipped from Sheet 23–1 into a priority ranking from most important to least important. Remember, you are trying to persuade an audience of contemporary parents that there are possible dangers for children in the future based on what occurred in the past. After you have done this, draw on the information to write a final essay for your audience on a separate piece of paper. Hand in both the final essay and this reorganized material.

Session 24. WHAT'S THE BEST ORDER?

Students have been experimenting with different ways to organize information. In this session, they decide for different situations which of the four patterns (alphanumeric, chronological, categorical, or in order of importance) is best.

OBJECTIVE

The students will identify organizational patterns appropriate to a situation.

SETTING THE STAGE

Knowing different ways to organize information is helpful only if students can apply the *right* organizational pattern. This exercise helps students think about applying an organizational pattern to a specific requirement.

PROCEDURE

1. Explain to students that they need to begin thinking about in what situations they should apply the different organizational patterns.
2. Hand out Sheet 24–1, "What's the Best Way to Order Information?," which asks students to choose from the multiple choices which organizational pattern is best for ten situations.

ANSWERS

1. B		6. C	
2. C		7. A (or B)	
3. D		8. C	
4. B		9. C (or A)	
5. D		10. A	

Name _____   Date _____

24–1. WHAT'S THE BEST WAY TO ORDER INFORMATION?

Directions: Ten situations are listed below. Circle the letter for the most appropriate organizational pattern for each situation.

1. You are writing instructions for a new cook to make a special meal.
   - a. alphanumerically
   - b. chronologically
   - c. by category
   - d. by priority

2. You are writing an overview to help a person who has not used a computer much to work on a complex computer system. The person will use the system in many different ways, using a variety of command sequences.
   - a. alphanumerically
   - b. chronologically
   - c. by category
   - d. by priority

3. You work in a large company, and you are writing a report for your busy boss about a new opportunity you have discovered
   - a. alphanumerically
   - b. chronologically
   - c. by category
   - d. by priority

4. You are writing a report for your busy boss about whom to meet, where to meet them, and topics for discussion on a three-day trip.
   - a. alphanumerically
   - b. chronologically
   - c. by category
   - d. by priority

5. You are writing to a large audience to motivate people to attend a fundraising event.
   - a. alphanumerically
   - b. chronologically
   - c. by category
   - d. by priority

6. You are writing a proposal to the president of a company to recommend the start of a new project.
   - a. alphanumerically
   - b. chronologically
   - c. by category
   - d. by priority

7. The president of the company gives you the go-ahead to start a new project. Now you have to tell everyone on your team what to do.
   - a. alphanumerically
   - b. chronologically
   - c. by category
   - d. by priority

8. You are trying to persuade an uninterested audience to change to a more healthful diet.
   - a. alphanumerically
   - b. chronologically
   - c. by category
   - d. by priority

9. You are listing healthful foods and calories for a group of dieters.
   - a. alphanumerically
   - b. chronologically
   - c. by category
   - d. by priority

10. You are listing class standings for your students.
    - a. alphanumerically
    - b. chronologically
    - c. by category
    - d. by priority

Session 25. CUTTING AND PASTING INDIVIDUAL WORK INTO A TEAM PIECE

In this exercise, students produce a team paper by cutting and pasting together elements from individual team members' work. This session helps students evaluate material, choose among alternatives, and develop negotiating skills. It also helps students focus on the language used to express an idea.

OBJECTIVES

The students will

- Analyze alternative solutions
- Develop team communications skills
- Create a simple team document

SETTING THE STAGE

The same cutting and pasting technique that students can use to revise their own work can also be used to create a team document. In fact, in the workplace and elsewhere, cutting and pasting individual work into a team piece is often used to

- Consolidate information from various team members
- Consolidate information from progress reports
- Create overviews

Team documents are particularly useful for keeping all members of the team informed and on track and for reporting to others what the team is doing.

By creating a team document, team members also learn to read a team document better. They learn that some information has been cut out, so they are seeing a partial story.

PROCEDURE

1. Group students into small teams of at least three members each.
2. Hand out Sheet 25–1, "Cutting and Pasting as a Team," to each student. Each team should select a topic as directed by the sheet,

without discussing the topic in any detail as a team or dividing up their coverage of it.

3. Each member of the team should then independently write approximately 300 words on the topic selected. Students may write essays, bulleted summaries, or a combination of formats as they see fit.

4. If you can, collect the work and photocopy the papers. Return originals to the students.

5. Regroup students and have each team create a team paper by cutting and pasting together sections from individual team members' work. No new material can be added, and the final work cannot exceed 500 words.

6. Evaluate the papers on the basis of organization and ideas in the final work. Do not consider style. You may want to look at the individual papers to see what was selected from each student.

7. Save the team papers for use in Session 26, "Polishing the Team's Work."

25–1. CUTTING AND PASTING AS A TEAM

Follow the directions on this sheet to see how your group can create a team document from the work of individuals.

1. In your group, decide on one of the following topics:

   • The emerging role of women in society

     The audience: the members of an all-male club

     The objective: to open club admission to women

   • What the family will be like in the future

     The audience: single, young adults without children

     The objective: to stimulate thinking about relationships

   • Whether people will work more at home or in the office in the future

     The audience: people who sell office space

     The objective: to prepare them for the future

2. Do not discuss the topic in your group or divide it up between group members in any way.

3. Each member of the group writes a 300-word piece (essay or bulleted summary or combination thereof) on the topic, working completely independently. Leave space between sections or paragraphs so they can be easily cut and pasted later.

4. Once you have everyone's finished piece and the teacher's go-ahead, select at least one paragraph from each member's work and paste it into the group's document. You can use more than one paragraph from any member. Make your document as stimulating and logical as possible, without adding or editing—you can only cut and paste. The final work must not exceed 500 words.

Session 26. POLISHING THE TEAM'S WORK

Polishing the team's work from the previous session is an excellent exercise in editing. Individual students must refrain from reinserting their own ideas and biases to be fair to the team. They must also learn to contribute to the work of the whole and to accept compromise.

OBJECTIVES

The students will

- Revise creatively within tight constraints
- Present a team's ideas

SETTING THE STAGE

Working in a team can be difficult, especially when you have to subordinate your own ideas to what the group has decided. Not all of a student's ideas may have been put into the team's work (a situation that happens repeatedly whenever people work together).

This exercise, therefore, is a challenge. Students have to be fair to the team's ideas, and that requires objectivity. Once they have experienced this detached objectivity, they may be better able to apply it to their own work.

PROCEDURE

1. Once the group essays from the previous session are handed in, you should evaluate them, making suggestions for improving or changing the work.

2. Make a photocopy of the team's work for each member of the team. Include on it the grade and your suggestions.

3. Hand out the photocopies (without regrouping teams) and write the following directions on the board:

   Your job is to revise the copy of your team's work to make the group look as good as possible. Make the work as concise as you can and edit it for continuity, style, and mechanics (as required by the format of the work). You must present all ideas in the team's work, but you may add new ideas for the sake of continuity. However, you may not add new ideas for any other purpose. Before beginning your draft, you may want to make notes and edit on the original. Your grade will be based on how well the final work reads, how accurately it represents the team's thinking, and how carefully it has been edited.

4. Warn students against reinserting their own ideas or changing the order of presentation of ideas in the original work.

5. Evaluate each student's revision individually, based on how well it reads, how accurately it represents the team, and how carefully it was edited.

Section 4

Presenting Information Visually

_____

PRESENTING INFORMATION VISUALLY

Stacey Cheng must give a speech. She has seen other speakers use visual aids for their speeches. She would like to use them, too, but she is not a graphic designer and doesn't know how to create visual aids herself. She knows visual aids would enhance her speech and help her audience focus on key points.

Stacey Cheng—and your students—can develop skills to think and communicate visually. These skills will serve them well in

- Making oral presentations
- Preparing illustrations to support text
- Creating videos

By learning these skills, students also learn to "read" visual information better—a necessary skill in our increasingly image-centered world.

Section Four contains eleven sessions that will help your students develop skills in communicating nonverbally, creating slides and transparencies, using storyboards and video, making statistics visual with graphs, and using "word pictures" in their writing.

Session 27. Is It What I Say, How I Say It, or How It Looks?

As students learned in Section One, most communication is oral. In this session, students learn that the *nonverbal* elements in communication are extremely important.

Session 28. The Art of Body Language

With their classmates' aid, students learn how to become more visually interesting when making a presentation by focusing on body language.

Session 29. Using Slides and Transparencies

To make a presentation more visually engaging, speakers can use slides or transparencies (also called "overheads" or "foils"). This exercise teaches students how to prepare these materials. It does not, however, require that you actually produce either slides or transparencies.

Session 30. Communicating Ideas with a Storyboard

In Session 29, students prepared storyboards without knowing it. In this session, students work with a storyboard to convey ideas visually.

Session 31. Developing an Idea Visually

Visual ideas can also be the starting point for projects, with text added later. In this session, students create a five-panel storyboard for a young child's birthday card, beginning with a visual idea.

Session 32. Communicating with Videos

This session introduces students to the video as a communication tool. They conceptualize and plan a video to promote their town, city, or state. No actual production of the video is necessary.

Session 33. Brainstorming a Four-Minute Video

Because most videos and films are actually conceptualized by teams, not individuals, in this session students work together to brainstorm ideas for a video that introduces their school to new students. Then they independently create a short treatment and storyboard for the video.

Session 34. Creating a Team Video Concept

In this session, students orally present to their teams the treatments and storyboards they developed in the previous session. The team then cuts and pastes together a final team treatment and storyboard for their video.

Session 35. Translating Statistics into Graphs

Graphs are another visual aid for effective communication. By turning raw statistics into visual images, graphs can make difficult material readily comprehensible. In this session, students learn about graphing information.

Session 36. What Does That Graph Really Mean?

Since graphs have become a popular way to represent complex and important data for decision making, students need to learn ways that graphs, data, and statistics can be manipulated. This exercise shows students how the same data can support different sides of an argument.

Session 37. Painting Word Pictures

Painting pictures with words is another way to make data more accessible. In a word picture, an abstract piece of data is related to a concrete measure that helps an audience visualize the magnitude of the data. For example, the White House at one time projected the budget deficit for 1991 to be $168.8 billion. If dollar bills were placed end to end, the resulting ribbon would encircle the earth and moon thirty-seven times! That's a word picture of the projected deficit. This session introduces students to creating their own word pictures.

Session 27. IS IT WHAT I SAY, HOW I SAY IT, OR HOW IT LOOKS?

Most communication is oral. In this session, students learn that the non-verbal elements in oral communication hold the audience's attention more than what is actually said.

OBJECTIVE

The students will analyze the importance of visual elements in communication.

SETTING THE STAGE

Every speech has three elements:

1. What is said—the message
2. How it is said—the emotion in the speaker's voice, the loudness, the pace
3. The way the presenter looks when saying it, including the speaker's gestures, body language, and eye contact

We normally focus most on getting the message right. We hone our words, revising the message until it sings on paper. Occasionally we work on how we sound. We rarely devote much thought to the purely visual elements—yet studies have found that the visual elements are by far the most important in holding an audience.

PROCEDURE

1. Discuss with students the three elements of an oral presentation, using the information in "Setting the Stage" above.
2. Hand out Sheet 27–1, "What Holds Your Interest Best?." Tell students you want them to help determine the most important area to work on in preparing a speech.
3. Collect the completed sheets and immediately tell students they need an exercise break. As you demonstrate each action, tell them to

   a. Stretch their arms out
   b. Reach up

   c. Wiggle their fingers in the air

   d. Sway left and right

   e. Hang their arms loose at their sides

   f. Reach forward

   g. Touch their chin with both hands (but you should touch your cheeks rather than your chin)

Carefully look at the class, and give them time to look at one another. Usually a large number of students will have put their hands on their cheeks, ignoring the instruction.

4. Use this result and students' responses to Sheet 27–1 as the basis for discussing the elements of oral presentations. Don't grade the sheet. Tell students that research suggests that the correct answers for question 4 are

    __3__ Verbal __7%__

    __2__ Vocal __30%__

    __1__ Visual __63%__

5. Students may be surprised by the importance of the visual element in comparison to the other two. Have them identify speeches they've seen and heard and share their recollections. Do they remember what was said? Can they quote anything verbatim? Do they remember how it was said? Do they remember how it looked? Most people will remember best how the speaker looked.

6. Remind students that communication is based on a connection between at least two people. Unless they stay connected, the communication will fail. Visual elements help keep people connected.

Name _____   Date _____

27–1. WHAT HOLDS YOUR INTEREST BEST?

Directions: Answer the following questions by circling the letter of the response that comes closest to your opinion.

1. During a typical day, which of the following do you do most?
   a. Look at what is going on around you
   b. Listen to what is going on around you
   c. Talk about what is going on around you

2. Which communication skill did primitive people develop first?
   a. The ability to talk with others
   b. The ability to see
   c. The ability to write

3. When someone is speaking, what involves you most?
   a. What the person is saying
   b. How the person is saying it
   c. How the person looks and moves

4. Researchers have measured the effects of verbal (what is said), vocal (how it is said), and visual (how the speaker looks presenting the message) elements on audiences. They have measured what penetrates the most and what involves the audience the most. Number the elements in terms of importance (with one being most important). To the right of each element, estimate its percentage of importance to a typical audience.

   _____ Verbal _____

   _____ Vocal _____

   _____ Visual _____

5. Describe a speech you witnessed in person and liked. (Try to use a non-school speech.) What do you remember about the event?

   _____

   _____

   _____

   _____

   _____

   _____

Session 28. THE ART OF BODY LANGUAGE

In the previous session, students learned that how a presenter *looks* is very important. In this session, classmates help students learn how to become more visually interesting when making a presentation by focusing on their body language.

OBJECTIVES

The students will

- Define body language
- Develop skills to make a presentation more visually engaging

SETTING THE STAGE

Talking in a meeting or before a small group is terrifying to many people. Learning some presentation skills and practicing in small groups will lessen this fear and promote more effective speaking before audiences, both large and small.

PROCEDURE

1. Hand out Sheet 28–1, "Holding an Audience's Attention," and Sheet 28–2, "Body Language." Conduct a discussion of body language as a communication tool. Have students define body language on Sheet 28–2 and see how many examples they can list. Collect the Sheet 28–2 for use on the next day.

2. Ask students to prepare for the next day a short (two-minute) talk in which they describe what they see themselves doing on a typical day ten years from now. Encourage them to practice their presentations in front of a mirror at home, if possible, but to avoid theatrics. Be sure to tell them that they will be making their presentations only to a small group of students in the class (or you may have some extra absentees!).

3. At the start of class, divide the students into small teams of no more than four students. Redistribute Sheet 28–2, "Body Language," and tell students they are to list specific examples of body language that assist communication as they watch the speakers in their team.

4. Organize groups in different parts of the room by having each group place their desks in a semicircle in front of which the speaker can

stand. If your classroom does not allow this, you may want to consider changing the exercise to eliminate teams, instead having each student talk to the whole class.

5. Before the presentations begin, inform the class that they will be asked to share with the speakers in their own team what worked effectively in their body language. Remind them that this assignment is very difficult because it leaves the presenter vulnerable to criticism. Stress kindness.

6. Have each team member, in turn, make a presentation, followed by a short comment period. Remind students to pay more attention to the way the presenter acts than to what he or she says.

7. When all presentations are complete, discuss with the class their experiences. To relieve tension, ask them to begin by discussing what it felt like to present. Was it as bad as they had expected? Was it difficult to use their hands and smile during the presentation? Ask for volunteers to share with the class tips they gleaned for effective body language. These should be added to the other students' lists.

28–1. HOLDING AN AUDIENCE'S ATTENTION

1. *Make eye contact with the audience.*

   • No other tip is as important

   • Look right at people. You're talking to individuals—engage them as individuals with your eyes.

   • If you are speaking to a large room of people,

     – Shift your eye contact from area to area.

     – Make contact with a specific person in each area.

2. *Use gestures (moving hands and arms) to add emphasis.*

   • Try to use palm up, open-handed gestures.

     – If you bend down and point at a dog, it will back away. Open your hand and it will approach. An audience is the same.

   • Don't "talk with your hands."

     – Don't let your hands become the focus of the presentation.

3. *Model the behavior you want in your audience.*

   • For example, when you ask, "Are there any questions?" raise your own hand immediately.

4. *Use as much space as you have.*

   • If you can move about, do so.

   • When practicing your presentation, try reaching up and out toward your audience.

5. *Watch excellent speakers.*

   • Pay attention to their body language.

   • Mimic their motions when you speak.

6. *Be enthusiastic.*

   • Excitement is contagious, as is boredom.

   • You can't excite your audience unless you're excited.

7. *Smile!*

28–2. BODY LANGUAGE

1. Define body language: _____

    _____

    _____

2. List types of body language: _____

    _____

    _____

    _____

Directions: As each person stands to tell you about his or her day in the future, watch the way he or she presents. List below specific examples of body language that you found effective.

1. _____

2. _____

3. _____

4. _____

5. _____

6. _____

7. _____

8. _____

9. _____

10. _____

Session 29. USING SLIDES AND TRANSPARENCIES

To make a presentation more visually engaging, a speaker can use slides or transparencies (also called "overheads" or "foils"). This exercise teaches students how to prepare and use these support materials. However, it does not require that you actually produce slides or transparencies.

OBJECTIVES

The students will

• Analyze material to identify central ideas
• Create text for slides and transparencies

SETTING THE STAGE

Transparencies are usually 8½″ × 11″ in size and work with an overhead projector. Most can be made on a standard photocopying machine, using special films. They can be used in a lit room, and you can write on them.

Slides require special photographic equipment to produce. While they have better graphic quality than transparencies, they can only be used in a darkened room and they cannot be written on during the presentation.

Material for production of both slides and transparencies is prepared in exactly the same way. First, the written material is drafted and sketched (or "dummied"). Actual production depends on how sophisticated your graphic requirements are.

The most important point to remember is that these materials are created to *support* a presentation. The presentation should not revolve around the slides or transparencies. Sheet 29–1, "Tips for Creating Visual Supports," provides more information on this.

As students become more conversant with this new skill, they can try to make foils and slides that employ images that *indirectly* touch on or support the subject. (See the example of the magazine mastheads included later in this section.)

PROCEDURE

1. If possible, use a photocopying machine to create transparencies from the three full-page examples provided after Sheet 29–1. Schedule an overhead projector for class if you don't already have one.

2. Your class may not be familiar with transparencies and slides. Take a few minutes to introduce them, holding up any examples you might have. Distinguish for your class between creating material that will

appear in such displays and actually producing them. The box in example 1 shows rough material that might be submitted by a writer, while the larger type shows how that material was translated by a graphic designer.

3. Hand out Sheet 29–1, "Tips for Creating Visual Supports," and go over it with the class as you display the examples on the projector. Example 1 illustrates the first three tips, and example 2 the fourth tip. Example 3 (magazine mastheads) is an example of indirect visual support. Instead of directly relating to the talk, it shows magazine mastheads to give listeners a "feel" for the topic.

4. Hand out Sheet 29–2, "Script for a Presentation," and Sheet 29–3, "Transparency Worksheet." Tell the class to follow the directions to prepare transparencies supporting the presentation script provided. Remind them to keep it simple.

5. Collect the work. If time permits, produce actual transparencies from examples of good (concise) and poor (verbose) drafts. When you project them, the class will readily see the difference. Discuss why some are better than others.

ANSWERS

Answers will vary, of course. One solution is shown below:

Transparency 1. *A Better Summer for YOU*

Transparency 2. *A beautiful outdoor camp*

- Sparkling lake
- Horseback riding
- Hiking

Transparency 3. *The job*

- Help youngsters, ages ten to twelve
- Needed: instructors, counselors, kitchen help
- Work ten full weeks

Transparency 4. *What you get*

- Free transportation, food, and lodging
- Time to enjoy camp's facilities
- $2,500

Transparency 5. *Fromm, Inc.*

- Twenty-five years serving youngsters
- Award-winning programs
- Fifteen camps in six states

29–1. TIPS FOR CREATING VISUAL SUPPORTS

The most important point to remember is that slides and transparencies *support* a presentation. The presentation should not revolve around them; the speaker should remain the focus.

With that major point in mind, here are some tips for drafting material for slides and transparencies:

1. Identify only the central ideas or key phrases in material.

2. Never put more than three ideas on a slide; preferably, use only one.

3. Choose material to help you engage the audience—don't display your presentation word for word. (If you want your audience to have exact wording of key parts, prepare notes and hand them out after the presentation.)

4. Follow the KISS principle (Keep it Simple, Stupid!). Use as few words as possible.

5. Try to use lists, not text—and make sure the elements in them are gramatically parallel.

6. Limit the number of displays. A general rule is to use one display per minute. You can use one for more than a minute, but avoid projecting one for less. If you use too many, you will focus the audience on your dexterity in changing displays instead of on your presentation.

7. The first display should simply help the audience adjust to your use of displays. It should be projected as you begin and say little, if anything.

Use techniques you learned for writing bulleted summaries: headings, visual elements (bullets, asterisks, dashes, boldface, underlining, italics, etc.), and good use of white space.

As you become more familiar with displays, you can make them more interesting by adding color, graphics, photographs, or images from newspapers and magazines.

- # Only Central Ideas
- # Three Ideas—MAX
- # NOT Verbatim

Original rough material:
- Only central ideas
- Three ideas—MAX
- NOT verbatim

KEEP IT SIMPLE, STUPID! (KISS)

EXAMPLE 3: FOR A TALK ABOUT MAGAZINES

Name _____   Date _____

29–2. SCRIPT FOR A PRESENTATION

Directions: Below you will find the script for a short oral presentation about a fictitious summer job program and the opportunities it offers high school students. Underline key points for an audience of high school students interested in learning more about the opportunity.

Are your summers usually boring? Do you stay at home? If you have a job, do you work inside? Are you given the worst jobs? If you want to work outdoors this summer, get away from home, take on some responsibility, and make some money, we want to talk to you.

Hi! My name is Tracy Biers and I'm with a company called Fromm, Inc. If you have a few minutes, I want to tell you about a different kind of summer job. You can work in a beautiful outdoor camp. The site offers a sparkling lake for canoeing, sailing, swimming, and even fishing. There's horesback riding and hiking trails.

Let me tell you about the job. We're looking for people to help youngsters, ages ten through twelve, enjoy this site to the fullest. We're looking for instructors, counselors, and kitchen help. You'll work about eight hours a day, six days a week, for ten full weeks. You'll get as much responsibility as you can handle.

Here's what you'll get. We will pay your way to and from the campsite. You will receive free food and lodging. Most of the time, you won't work eight hours straight, so you'll have time off to enjoy the campsite's facilities yourself. At the end of ten weeks, we'll pay you with a check for $2,500.

Now let me tell you about the company, Fromm, Inc. We have been in business for more than twenty-five years serving youngsters. We have tested and developed an outstanding, summer-long program that has won awards for excellence. We run fifteen camps in six states during the summer.

It's an exciting opportunity for your summer. If you're interested, let's talk. Thank you.

29—3. TRANSPARENCY WORKSHEET

Directions: Create up to six transparencies to support the oral presentation script you were given. Each box should contain text for one transparency. Try to be as brief as possible. Remember that the first transparency should show little, if anything, so the audience can adjust to your use of displays. You can use headings, lists, and other visual elements in each transparency. Make sure you use parallel construction throughout the presentation. Do not concern yourself with how the transparencies will be produced.

1.

2.

3.

4.

5.

6.

Session 30. COMMUNICATING VISUAL IDEAS WITH A STORYBOARD

In Session 29, students prepared storyboards without knowing that was what they were doing. A storyboard is a handy way to deal with visual ideas before they are produced. In this session, students learn how to use a storyboard to design visual images to accompany an oral presentation.

OBJECTIVE

The students will develop storyboarding skills.

SETTING THE STAGE

In the previous session, photos and graphics would have enlivened the presentation of the camping opportunity. Pictures, cartoons, photos, and graphics can make any text material (brochures, papers, magazines, or transparencies) more engaging. If you are not a skilled artist, however, how do you convey your ideas about what you want visually?

The answer is to use a storyboard and then turn your visual ideas over to a graphic designer to produce (unless you can do it yourself). A storyboard is simply a series of boxes that tell a story in pictures. It is rarely (if ever) self-standing. It is supported by text and people talking about what they envision. It can be very simple or a work of art.

PROCEDURE

1. Hand out Sheet 29–2, "Script for a Presentation," which you may have collected from the students after the previous session, or you may need to photocopy again.
2. Hand out Sheet 30–1, "Storyboarding the Job Script," and go through it with the students. It takes them step-by-step through the production of a storyboard to accompany the script on Sheet 29–2.
3. Hand out Sheet 30–2, "Completing the Storyboard," which asks students to come up with two possibilities for each of the last two frames of the storyboard. Encourage students to think visually.
4. Collect the work.

ANSWERS

Possible visuals for the fourth transparency, about pay, are

- A check for $2,500
- A student receiving a check
- Students relaxing by the lake
- Students partying
- A youngster shaking hands and saying goodbye to a student

Possible visuals for the fifth transparency, about the company, are

- The company headquarters
- The awards the company has won
- The company president shaking hands with students
- A map showing states where the company has sites

30–1. STORYBOARDING THE JOB SCRIPT

A *storyboard* is a series of boxes that visually tell a story. It is used to organize visual ideas and explain them to others before they are actually produced by an artist or graphic designer. The simplest storyboard doesn't even need to have drawings—you just indicate the need for a visual element and describe it. Most do have drawings, however.

Find your copy of the "Script for a Presentation." We are going to add visuals to the camping job presentation. Remember that each transparency should remain projected for at least thirty seconds, so you don't want more than about five transparencies for this short presentation.

TRANSPARENCY 1

The first transparency promises a better summer for students. What visual image can you show instead of simply writing the text? One image is a student looking bored. To indicate this visual, you write "bored student" in brackets in the box. You can sketch the student if you like, but it is not required.

[photo: bored student]

TRANSPARENCY 2

The second transparency supports material about the campsite. How do you show the campsite? You could use an aerial photo of the campground, a photo of the entrance to the camp, the lake, a sailboat on the lake, a group hiking, or someone fishing or horseback riding. That is a lot of photographs. You might want to make this transparency a *montage* of separate visuals brought together. Used sparingly, this is an effective technique.

THE CAMP-SITE . . . [photo: campsite entrance]	A SPARKLING LAKE . . . [photo: lake]
HORSEBACK RIDING . . . [photo: horseback group on trail]	HIKING . . . [photo: group hiking]

TRANSPARENCY 3

The third transparency could present the job. The job is explained in various ways. You could use a montage, but is it needed? You don't want to have too many. Is there a single visual that might engage the audience? You might try a single photo of a high school employee working with a group of youngsters.

THE JOB . . . • Work with youngsters • Needed: instructors, counselors, kitchen help • 10 weeks [photo: high school student working with youngsters

The graphic artist will decide how to integrate the text with the photograph. Sometimes the photos or graphics can be so strong that you can eliminate some or all of the text.

Now you will finish the storyboard, on a separate exercise sheet.

Name _____ Date _____

30–2. COMPLETING THE STORYBOARD

Directions: Use Sheet 29–2, "Script for a Presentation," and Sheet 30–1, "Storyboarding the Job Script," to help you complete the storyboard for the camping job presentation. There is time for two more transparencies:

• Transparency 4 is about what the job pays.
• Transparency 5 is about the company.

What images could suggest the pay or the company? See the script for clues. Then come up with two possibilities for each of the transparencies and explain them or sketch them in the boxes below. Use capital letters for text that you want to appear on the finished transparencies. Write any instructions for the graphic artist in brackets [ ].

TRANSPARENCY 4

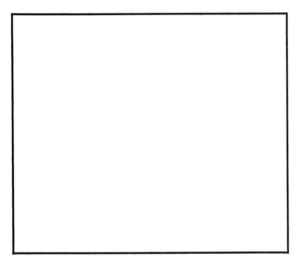

Note: The capitalized text will be retained in the final work.

TRANSPARENCY 5

Note: The capitalized text will be retained in the final work.

Session 31. DEVELOPING AN IDEA VISUALLY

So far, students have learned to add visuals in support of text. However, visual ideas can also be the starting point for projects, with the text added later. In this session, students create a five-panel storyboard for a child's birthday card, beginning with a visual idea.

OBJECTIVE

The students will develop a project from a visual idea.

SETTING THE STAGE

Sometimes communication *begins* with a rough storyboard. Cards, invitations, brochures, advertisements, billboards, and packaging often begin as a storyboard. In these cases, the visual ideas rather than the text drive the project. In some cases, there may be no text at all.

You don't have to be an artist to create a storyboard; stick figures will do. These rough sketches are merely meant to help others visualize the project. What matters is not the quality of the drawing, but the quality of the visual idea.

PROCEDURE

1. You may want to make transparencies or photocopies of examples 1 and 2, full-page sheets that follow this section. They show both the storyboard and the finished product for an invitation to the announcement of a new software product. This invitation was built on the visual idea of linking the development of people from babies to children to adults with the development of computer use from individual applications to sophisticated networking.

2. Explain to the class that projects can begin with visual ideas. Show them the rough storyboard example and the final product (you might want to explain that the bottom panel unfolds from the opened card).

3. Tell students that they will be creating a rough storyboard for a five-panel birthday card for a five-year-old. Five panels are used so students will have to conceptualize a small story in visual terms.

4. Hand out Sheet 31–1, "Designing a Card for a Young Child." Go over the assignment with students and provide them with scrap paper for initial doodling (if they want to use anything from their doodles, they can paste it to the sheet). They should work in pencil

and ignore colors for now. They can include text in each panel, if it should appear on the final page. When they are done sketching the entire sequence, they should briefly write under each page what they are trying to show.

5. Evaluate the work for the visual concept, not the quality of the drawing.

EXAMPLE 1: ROUGH STORYBOARD FOR AN INVITATION

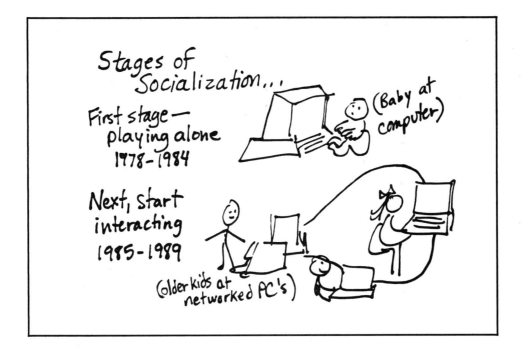

EXAMPLE 2: FINAL PIECE PRODUCED BY ARTIST

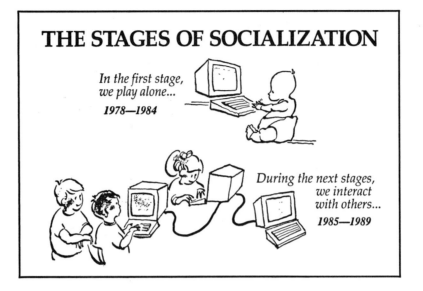

Art by Paul Schulenburg

31–1. DESIGNING A CARD FOR A YOUNG CHILD

Directions: Your job is to sketch a rough storyboard for a five-panel birthday card for a five-year-old boy or girl. Since few five-year-olds read well, this needs to be a visually oriented sequence. You can add simple text if you want it to appear on the page. Although a parent may read the card to the child, it should be geared toward the child's understanding. When you are done with the entire card, briefly describe under each box what you are trying to show. *Hint:* Start doodling on scrap paper before drawing on this sheet.

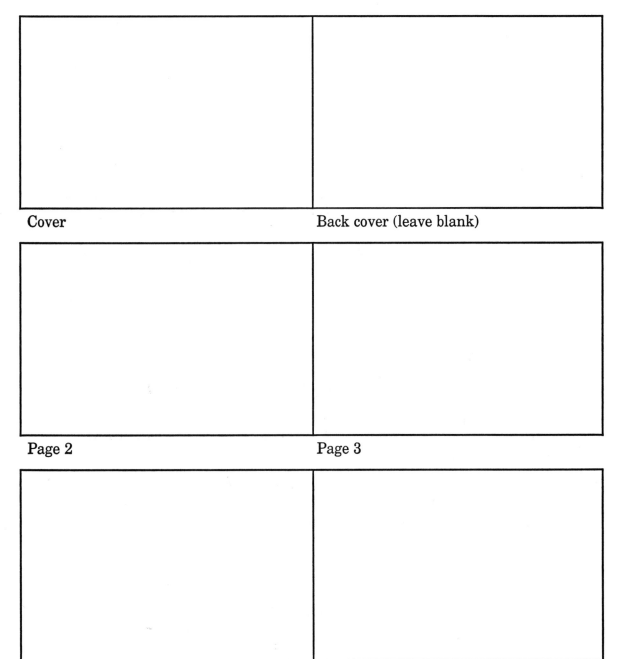

Cover   Back cover (leave blank)

Page 2   Page 3

Page 4   Page 5

Session 32. COMMUNICATING WITH VIDEOS

This session introduces students to the video as a communication tool. They conceptualize and plan a video; however, there is no need to produce the video.

OBJECTIVES

The students will

- Relate video to other types of communication
- Create a plan, or treatment, for a short video

SETTING THE STAGE

The video is a popular communication medium. It plays an obvious role in television news and entertainment; however, it is also increasingly used in business, government, and education to communicate information. Consider the growing use of "video yearbooks" in high schools.

Video adds another dimension to the word and image: motion. Your students will probably not have to be convinced of the importance of video as a communication medium, but they may not have given much thought to how one is made.

A video begins with planning in the form of a treatment and a storyboard. Storyboards for video and film use the same format already presented in previous sessions. For full-length films, artists draw storyboards that can include more than fifty individual boards and cost more than $100,000.

A treatment is a brief, written description of the video (or film), including statements on the proposed audience, objective, duration (length), and content (concept). Usually, only after all involved parties agree on the video treatment are storyboards drawn, scripts written, and production begun.

PROCEDURE

1. Begin the class by asking students how they visualize a video. Use brainstorming techniques for about five minutes. Usually, students talk about video techniques, background music, what people wear on camera, and special effects. After about five minutes, stop the discussion and ask, "Who's the audience? What's the objective?"

2. Tell students a video is like all other communication media: Before you can deliver a message, you need to define the audience and

160

objective. Using the information in "Setting the Stage," introduce them to the idea of video treatment.

3. Hand out Sheet 32–1, "Example of a Treatment," and discuss how it conveys the concept of the video.

4. Distribute Sheet 32–2, "Develop a Video Treatment." Explain that students are to write a treatment for a short video that will be submitted to a contest for secondary school students. The video should focus on their town, city, or state. The audience is the city council public affairs commission, and the objective is to promote the city (or town or state).

32-1. EXAMPLE OF A TREATMENT

AUDIENCE

People with at least a high school education who are broadly familiar with the American colonies' fight for independence from Great Britain.

OBJECTIVE

To provide a sense of how it felt to live through the American Revolution.

THE CONCEPT

Most Americans are familiar with the fight for our independence. They know the names of famous patriots and sites of battles. They know about the Declaration of Independence and Liberty Hall. Few, however, have any idea what living through those days felt like.

To give a sense of the revolutionary experience, we will film locations where key events occurred. We will also use paintings and sketches of events. Off-camera narrators will read the preserved letters and diaries of soldiers, farmers, merchants, and other common people who actually experienced the revolution. Their voices will tell the tale.

To augment these personal views, we will show brief on-camera interviews with leading scholars in Revolutionary period history.

We will also blend in video of period pieces, such as furniture, preserved newspapers, and flags. We will record period music, including marching and popular songs.

VIEWING TIME

Three hours, divided into three parts.

32–2. DEVELOP A VIDEO TREATMENT

A treatment is: ———————————————————————————————
——

Directions: Write a treatment below for a short video that is supposed to promote your town, city, or state as part of a contest run by a government public affairs commission. The contest is open to secondary school students. Remember to write the concept concisely.

Audience: ——————————————————————————————————
——

Objective: ——————————————————————————————————
——
——

Concept: ———————————————————————————————————
——
——
——
——
——
——
——
——
——
——
——

Viewing Time: ————————————————————————————————

Session 33. BRAINSTORMING A FOUR-MINUTE VIDEO

Most videos and films are conceptualized by a team. In this session, student teams brainstorm ideas for a video that introduces their school to new students. They then work alone to develop a short treatment and storyboard.

OBJECTIVES

The students will

- Brainstorm, in a team, ideas for a short video
- Create a treatment and storyboard independently using the team's ideas

SETTING THE STAGE

A team is ideal for conceptualizing a video or film. Just as a number of cameras allow you to record an event from different vantage points, the members of a team can offer many different perspectives on a project. In this session, students work together to conceptualize a video that introduces their school to new students.

Sheet 33–1, "Questions for Conceptualizing a School Video," lists a number of issues students may want to discuss, and students will generate more questions as they brainstorm. As the sheet tells students, a four-minute video can convey roughly eight ideas (one every thirty seconds).

PROCEDURE

1. Explain the assignment. The class will break into teams to brainstorm a four-minute video introducing their school to new students. After the brainstorming session, students will independently write a treatment and prepare a storyboard that will be turned in for evaluation.

2. Divide the class into teams and hand out Sheet 33–1, "Questions for Conceptualizing a School Video," Sheet 33–2, "Introducing My School: A Treatment," and Sheet 33–3, "Introducing My School: The Storyboard."

3. Using the Sheet 33–1, go over issues the groups should discuss. Encourage them to come up with more as they brainstorm. However, warn them that once they have explored possibilities, they need to focus on only a few issues. They must decide what is most important

to introduce new students to the school. Remind them not to discuss dialogue or actual wording for the video. Right now they are concentrating on the ideas they want to convey, not how to convey them.

4. Let the students brainstorm for twenty to thirty minutes.

5. For the rest of the period and homework, students work independently to prepare the treatment and storyboard. Remind students that the storyboard does not need to be great art, just rough sketching.

6. As you grade the work, remember the objective is to introduce new students to the school.

33–1. QUESTIONS FOR CONCEPTUALIZING A SCHOOL VIDEO

Below is a list of questions your group should consider as you brainstorm ideas for a four-minute video introducing your school to new students. You will undoubtedly want to come up with other questions as well. Remember, however, that a four-minute video can effectively present only eight ideas (one for each thirty seconds). Of all the ideas your group generates, which should your video focus on?

- From whose viewpoint will the story be told? A student's? Teacher's? Principal's? Parent's? New student's?

- What aspects of the school will you show? Its regular academic program? Sports? Drama?

- What messages about the school do you want to deliver?

- What will you say about the school's academic standards?

- Do you want to tell what happens to graduates (where they go)?

- Do you want to present the school's history?

- Has the school won any awards? Received state or national recognition?

- Will you show any special programs?

- Will you show counselors, psychologists, or anyone else providing special services?

- Can you use any existing video? Do you have any of sports events (football games, baseball games)?

- Will you show any textbooks?

- What areas of the school building will you show?

- Will you show the cafeteria?

33–2. INTRODUCING MY SCHOOL: THE TREATMENT

Directions: Write a treatment for a four-minute video that will introduce your school to new students.

The audience: _____
_____

The objective: _____
_____
_____

Your concept: _____
_____
_____
_____
_____
_____
_____
_____
_____
_____
_____
_____
_____
_____
_____

Name _____ **Date** _____

33–3. INTRODUCING MY SCHOOL: THE STORYBOARD

Directions: Use the boxes below to sketch what you have in mind for your video. Each box represents about thirty seconds of viewing time. Under each box, write a brief description of what you are trying to show.

1.

2.

3

4.

5.

6.

7.

8.

Session 34. CREATING A TEAM VIDEO CONCEPT

A treatment and storyboard are designed to *support* the presentation of a video concept. In this session, students orally present to their teams the treatments and storyboards they developed individually in the previous session. Then the team cuts and pastes together a final treatment and storyboard.

OBJECTIVES

The students will

- Practice presentation skills
- Work as a team to cut and paste together a video treatment and storyboard

SETTING THE STAGE

A treatment and storyboard are only snapshots of how a person sees a film or video project, leaving out much of what was envisioned. An oral presentation allows the person to provide more details of that vision.

To be effective, the presentation should be made with excitement and enthusiasm, as well as careful attention to body language. The presenter should be prepared to answer any questions others may have about the concept.

In their presentations, students should begin with an overview of the entire video and then examine segments in more detail. Students on the team should hold their questions until the end of each presentation.

PROCEDURE

1. Make certain students have their completed individual treatments and storyboards from the previous session. Since they will be cutting and pasting them, make sure you have completed any necessary evaluation of the individual materials.
2. After explaining the assignment, allow students about ten minutes to prepare their oral presentations to their teams. Explain that this will be the same team they brainstormed ideas for the video with. Remind students to concentrate on effective oral communication skills—hold a quick review if necessary.

3. Reconvene the teams from the previous session and allow each student about five minutes to present. Urge the team to ask questions about the concepts when the presenter is finished. The more questions asked, the more likely it is that the student's concept will be understood fully.

4. When presentations are complete, hand out Sheet 34–1, "Introducing Our School: A Team Treatment," and Sheet 34–2, "Introducing Our School: A Team Storyboard." Instruct students to cut and paste together the best work of team members, adding new material if desired.

5. If you have time, you may want each team to present their final work to the whole class.

34–1. INTRODUCING OUR SCHOOL: A TEAM TREATMENT

Directions: Using the treatments prepared by the members of your team, identify the best ideas and cut and paste them together into a team treatment. You may add material if your discussion creates new ideas. Make certain that your treatment is coherent and consistent even though you are combining ideas from all team members.

The audience: _____

_____

The objective: _____

_____

_____

Your concept: _____

_____

_____

_____

_____

_____

_____

_____

_____

_____

_____

_____

Names _____

Date _____

34–2. INTRODUCING OUR SCHOOL: A TEAM STORYBOARD

Directions: Create the most interesting and effective video storyboard you can by combining the best ideas of the members of your team. You can create a new panel if the group's discussion generates new ideas.

5.

6.

7.

8.

Session 35. TRANSLATING STATISTICS INTO GRAPHS

By turning raw statistics into visual images, graphs can make difficult material more readily comprehensible. In this session, students learn about graphing data.

OBJECTIVE

The students will display data in various graph formats.

SETTING THE STAGE

To many people, *statistics* is a dirty word because they are difficult to understand and handle. But if you translate these seemingly incomprehensible statistics into a graph, they can suddenly communicate with clarity.

Six basic graph formats for the same data are illustrated on Sheet 35–1, "Different Types of Graphs":

- Line graph
- Shaded line graph
- Stacked bar graph
- Multiple lines graph
- Bar graph
- Pie chart

You can make a graph even more visually engaging by using pertinent images to represent the data. For example, if you are graphing the volume of oil imports, instead of drawing a bar you can draw oil barrels stacked on top of each other. Instead of just a pie chart of the United States' budget, you can make the whole chart a silver dollar.

PROCEDURE

1. Hand out Sheet 35–1, "Different Types of Graphs." Discuss the various kinds of graphs covered, and explore the use of appropriate images to make graphs more visually interesting.
2. Hand out Sheet 35–2, "Two Ways to Look at the Same Numbers." The sheet tabulates graduates at a fictitious high school. Each student graphs the same data in bar graph and line graph form. For each graph, students also suggest an image that represents the data. If you have access to any spreadsheet software, you can enter the data and allow students to experiment with the different graphs the program offers.
3. Collect and grade the work.

ANSWERS

The correct graphs are shown below.

BAR GRAPH: Graduates by Year

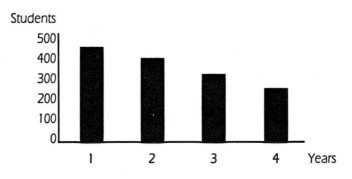

LINE GRAPH: Graduates by Year

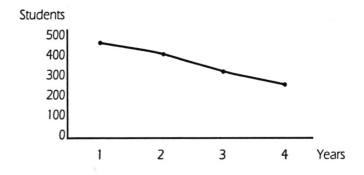

Possible graphics for the charts include

- Students in caps and gowns for bars
- A diploma under a line graph
- Diplomas for bars
- Stacked mortarboards for bars

35–1. DIFFERENT TYPES OF GRAPHS

Each graph shown is based on the following data:

High School Population				
	Year 1	**Year 2**	**Year 3**	**Year 4**
All classes	2,200	1,800	1,400	1,000
Freshman class	525	450	350	240

I. LINE GRAPH

Class Size by Year

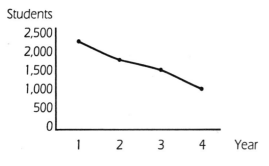

II. MULTIPLE LINES GRAPH

**Total Class Size Compared to
Freshman Class Size by Year**

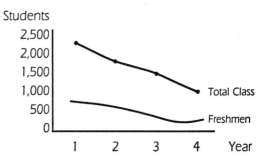

III. BAR GRAPH

Class Size by Year

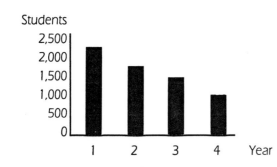

IV. SHADED LINE GRAPH

**Total Class Size Compared to
Freshman Class Size by Year**

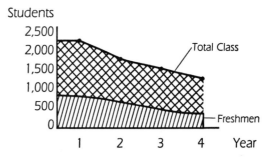

V. STACKED BAR GRAPH

**Freshman Class Size Plus
Other Classes by Year**

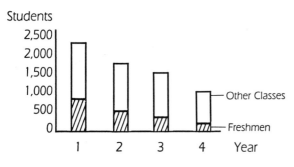

VI. PIE CHART

**Total Class Size Compared to
Freshman Class Size in Year 1**

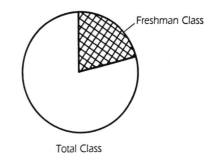

Name _____   Date _____

35–2. TWO WAYS TO LOOK AT THE SAME NUMBERS

Directions: The following table shows the number of students who have graduated from a fictitious high school over four years.

	Year 1	Year 2	Year 3	Year 4
Graduates	450	400	325	240

Graph the data as both a bar chart and a line graph. For each graph, suggest an image that would make the graph more visually interesting.

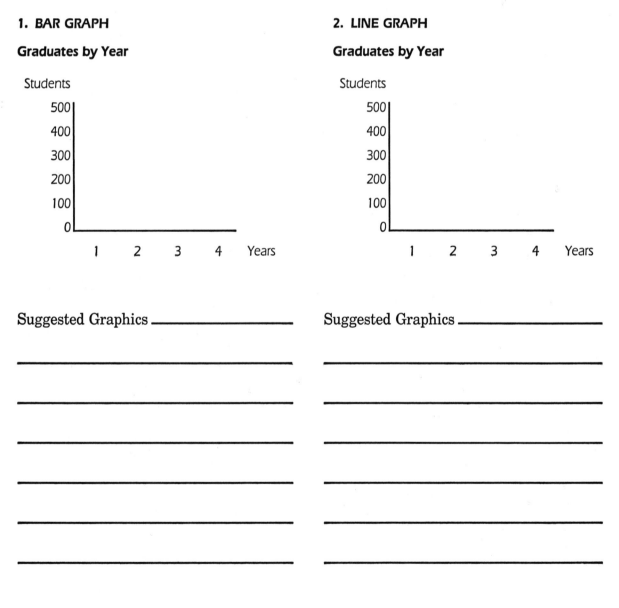

1. BAR GRAPH

Graduates by Year

Students

2. LINE GRAPH

Graduates by Year

Students

Suggested Graphics _____

_____

_____

_____

_____

_____

Suggested Graphics _____

_____

_____

_____

_____

_____

Session 36. WHAT DOES THAT GRAPH REALLY MEAN?

Since graphs are a popular way to represent complex and important data for decision making, it is important that students learn how data can be distorted by graphs and statistics. This exercise shows students how to use the same data to support two different sides of an argument.

OBJECTIVE

The students will analyze the graphic representation of data.

SETTING THE STAGE

Do statistics lie? No, but you can make them support just about any argument you like.

In today's world, graphs and statistics are used in politics, in business, in education—in just about every organization. A graph may catch your eye, but the wise person looks at the data behind the graph—even if it is hard to understand at first. This exercise shows students why it is important to look at the data.

PROCEDURE

1. Hand out Sheet 36–1, "This School Is Getting Worse—Or Is It?" Ask students to follow the directions to prepare two graphs from the same data, to support two opposing positions. The data concerns the number of graduates a high school produces over four years.

2. If your class has access to a scanner and/or graphics software, you can ask the class to find images for the graphs. Students can look in the program bank of images or, if you have a scanner, in magazines, books, and newspapers. Images can be selected from or scanned into the graphics software and duplicated, expanded, contracted, etc., within a graph.

ANSWERS

The graphs are fairly straightforward. Percentages for the second graph should be

Year 1—76%   Year 3—88%
Year 2—83%   Year 4—96%

Name _____   Date _____

36–1. THIS SCHOOL IS GETTING WORSE—OR IS IT?

Directions: The following table shows the number of freshmen who entered a high school as a class and the number of them that went on to graduate.

	Year 1	Year 2	Year 3	Year 4
Freshmen entering	525	450	350	250
Graduates	400	375	310	240

Assume an argument is raging about how well the school is doing. Both sides are using the same table to take opposing positions. How can this be?

One Side Says the School is Getting Worse.

This side makes a bar graph for the number of students graduating each year. Complete the graph for this side below:

BAR GRAPH: Graduates by Year

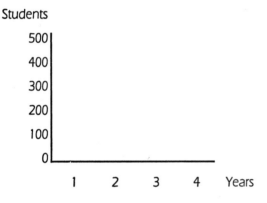

From the graph, it is plain that the school is producing fewer graduates each year. How could it be doing a good job?

But there's another side . . .

One Side Says the School is Getting Better.

This side has looked at the size of the incoming class and noticed that it is growing smaller. This side computed the percent of students graduating from each class. The formula for figuring this percentage is

$$\frac{\text{Number of graduates in a year}}{\text{Number of freshmen entering in the class}} \times 100 = \text{Graduation rate}$$

COMPUTE the percentage for each of the four years below:

	Year 1	Year 2	Year 3	Year 4
Graduation rate				

GRAPH the graduation rate by year as bars on the graph below:

BAR GRAPH: Graduation Rate by Year

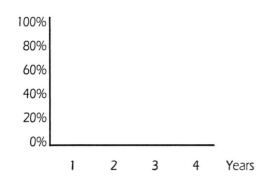

This side has taken a further step and asked a graphic designer to show the bars as graduates. The last graduate looks much bigger than the first. Relatively speaking, more students are graduating from each class. Clearly, the school is doing better.

Which side is correct? It all depends on how you want to use the data. But if you are an outsider, the best way to decide who is right is to look at the actual data and spend time analyzing it—and the issues—yourself.

Session 37. PAINTING WORD PICTURES

Painting pictures with words is another way to make data more accessible. In a word picture, an abstract piece of data is related to a concrete measure that helps the audience visualize the magnitude of the data. For example, the White House at one time projected the budget deficit for 1991 to be $168 billion. If that number of dollar bills were placed end to end, the resulting ribbon would encircle the earth and moon thirty-seven times! That is a word picture of the projected deficit. This session introduces students to creating their own word pictures.

OBJECTIVES

The students will

- Analyze apparently unrelated pieces of data
- Combine pieces of data into word pictures

SETTING THE STAGE

According to *Time* magazine, over the course of a lifetime, the average American will spend eight months sorting through junk mail. That is a word picture. It is easier to grasp than a statistic: In 1990, 63.7 billion pieces of junk mail were delivered.

Who thinks of these things? Anyone can. All you need is raw data and the willingness to plow through some basic math.

You'll find more examples of word pictures on Sheet 37–1, "Word Pictures."

PROCEDURE

1. Hand out Sheet 37–1, "Creating a Word Picture," and discuss the information on it with your class. Ask students if they can recall any other word pictures. Ask the class to use the sheet to create a word picture of their own. You may need to give students time in the library. Encourage them to skim through source material.
2. Collect the work, and share examples with the class.

ANSWERS

Word pictures for the number of federal employees might include the following:

- Find or estimate the height of an average American, and then multiply that distance by the number of employees. You could convert that distance from feet to miles. If there are enough employees, you can stack them feet on shoulders beyond the moon. Or, you can estimate the width of an average American with arms extended and then have Americans hold hands and ring the earth.
- Compare the number of people in the work force to the population of cities. For example, the number of federal employees might equal the number of people in New York, Los Angeles, Cleveland, and so on.
- Find the average number of people an American meets in a year and compute the number of years you would need to live to meet all the federal employees.

Word pictures for the golf course might include the following:

- Estimate the average distance walked to play one round of golf, convert the figure to miles, and find a comparable distance.
- Compute the number of times a golf ball fell into a cup (eighteen times per round played) and compare it to a person's heartbeat.

37–1. CREATING A WORD PICTURE

A *word picture* relates an abstract piece of data to a concrete measure that helps your audience visualize—and thereby comprehend—the magnitude of your data. Here are some examples:

- Let's say the United States budget deficit is projected to be $168.8 billion. If that many dollar bills were placed end to end, the resulting ribbon could encircle the earth and moon thirty-seven times!
- Here's another way to think of that $168.8 billion: If, back in 3377 B.C., the first Egyptian Pharaoh started spending one dollar each second, it would take until 1991 to finish spending $168.8 billion.
- According to *Time* magazine, over the course of a lifetime the average American spends eight months sorting through junk mail. (This is easier to grasp than the raw data that in 1990, 63.7 billion pieces of junk mail were delivered.)

Anyone can create these word pictures. All you need are sources of good data. The best sources can be found in your library. There you will find the raw data you need for comparisons—for example, the distance between the earth and the moon, the population of various cities, or the circumference of the earth. Some good sources are atlases, almanacs, encyclopedias, and the *Statistical Abstract of the United States.*

Directions: Go to the library and find the *Statistical Abstract of the United States* (it is often at the reference desk). Look up either

a. The total federal paid civilian employment figure (that is, the number of nonmilitary people who work for the federal government) for the most recent year available, OR

b. The total number of rounds of golf played in the United States for the most recent year. Or choose another sport. (See "Recreational Activities.")

Create a word picture for the piece of data you select:

_____

_____

_____

_____

_____

_____

Section 5

Presenting as an Organization: A Class Portrait

PRESENTING AS AN ORGANIZATION: A CLASS PORTRAIT

Patrick Jameson was the classic team player. He played football and baseball in high school. He worked well with teams in class. Everyone assumed he was the one person in class most likely to succeed, but his team skills failed him once he left the academic world.

What happened?

Patrick Jameson—like almost everyone else in the working world—is more than part of a team. He is part of a larger organization. Often, the ability to communicate with other parts of the organization is the key to success—and people who fail to develop the communication skills to work within organizations also fail to advance.

So far, students have learned to communicate as members of a team. But in larger organizations with codependent teams, each team not only performs its own job but must rely on other teams to perform theirs. Individuals are often judged by the whole organization's results.

In Section Five, students build on their new team communication skills to develop effective organizational communication skills. They work as a class to create a presentation for a special audience. This presentation will bring together most of the communication skills covered in this book. It will include an oral presentation by one group, a written report by another group, and support visuals created by another group.

The objective of the class will be to present a portrait of their attitudes and ideas about a controversial topic to a person or persons of your choice. You should plan to have your guests in class two weeks from when you begin the section. Some suggested guests include

- The school's administration
- Members of the board of education
- Parents

- A civic organization concerned with the topic
- Other classes
- Teachers in the school
- Teachers from other schools
- Members of the local chamber of commerce

Or, students could leave the school to present to a particular service organization or other group.

The portrait should reflect the range of attitudes in the class, but it should not try to convince the audience that one side is right or wrong about the issue.

You can structure the sessions in this section in many ways, but the section is designed to be used as a whole, with activities dovetailing into each other and working toward the final presentation.

You can stay within the class, but you can also work with classes in other subjects. For instance, a history or social studies class (or department teachers) could suggest possible topics and then be the audience for the presentation. An art class might be interested in producing the visual aids. A computer class might be interested in helping with other areas. Finally, your class could work with another class to gather data, painting the portrait not of itself but of another class. This interaction allows students to practice their listening skills.

Your class as a whole will brainstorm topics and decide on one that will serve as the focus of this project. Each student will write an essay on the topic to provide data for the portrait. In teams, the class will then categorize and organize the information into a fifteen- to twenty-page summary. Then it will break into four teams to handle the editing, polishing, visuals, and oral presentation, respectively. Sheet 38–1, "Flow Chart for a Class Portrait," presents a diagram of the entire process.

There are five sessions in Section Five. Note, however, that Session 41 has been broken down into four subsessions that run more or less concurrently as the various teams complete their part of the class portrait.

Session 38. Determining the Class Topic

In this session, the class brainstorms ideas for a topic for their presentation, aiming for something controversial that will be interesting to the audience and meaningful to the class.

Session 39. Snapping the Class Portrait

The organizational exercises in this section require data. Rather than devote time to research, students will generate the data themselves by writing individual essays that either define their personal position on the issue or describe the personal position of a student from another class.

Session 40. Organizing the Data

In this session, students work in groups and as a class to create categories and then organize their information accordingly. The final result will be a fifteen- to twenty-page summary.

Session 41. Producing the Portrait

This session consists of four separate sessions for the four separate groups. Enough activities are provided to keep all the students busy throughout the process.

Session 41A. The First Editing Team

This team edits the material provided in Session 40, concentrating on conciseness. It then serves as practice audience and coach to the oral presentation group.

Session 41B. The Second Editing Team

This team computes statistics while the first editing team does an initial edit. It then polishes the final written report and writes an introduction. It also works with the visuals team.

Session 41C. The Visuals Team

This team creates visuals to support the presentation—both transparencies for the oral presentation and illustrations for the written report.

Session 41D. The Oral Presentation Team

This team cooperates with other teams to prepare the oral presentation for the audience.

Session 42. Presenting the Portrait, and Review

The portrait is complete, and the class is ready to present. Once the presentation is over, you review the process with the class and consider improvements. This session allows you to review the variety of communication skills your students have developed.

Session 38. DETERMINING THE CLASS TOPIC

So far, students have learned to communicate as members of a team. In the two-week project covered in this section, they develop skills to work in larger organizations. In this session, the class learns about the project and brainstorms the topic for a presentation that should be both interesting to a special audience and meaningful to the class.

OBJECTIVES

The students will

- Analyze an audience
- Brainstorm topics for a class presentation

SETTING THE STAGE

In the workplace, most employees are called to work effectively not only in small teams, but also as members of a larger organization (the group, department, division, or corporation, for example). Especially in larger organizations, people may find themselves providing information for or actually making presentations on behalf of their groups to specialized audiences: corporate operations personnel, representatives of other divisions, potential clients or customers, the board of education, voters, and others. In the project that begins in this session, students experience some of the special challenges of working as part of a larger organization.

PROCEDURE

1. Hand out Sheet 38–1, "Flow Chart for a Class Portrait," and explain the entire project to the class:

    a. The class as a whole brainstorms topics and decides on one that will serve as the focus of their project.

    b. Each student writes a personal essay on the topic. (As an alternative, students might interview members of another class and write an essay defining those students' opinions.)

    c. The class consolidates individual essays into a class portrait, breaking into four teams to do the job.

    - Team 1 edits the document, making it accessible and concise.
    - Team 2 proofreads and polishes the material.

190

- Team 3 prepares visual supports.
- Team 4 prepares and delivers the oral presentation.

   d. The class as a whole participates in the presentation.

2. Identify the audience and date of presentation for your class. Some suggestions for guests are

- The school's administration
- Members of the board of education
- Parents
- A civic organization concerned with the topic
- Other classes
- Teachers in the school
- Teachers from other schools
- Members of the local chamber of commerce

3. Hand out Sheet 38–2, "Topic and Audience for a Class Portrait," which asks students to list topics of interest to them and answer questions about their selections on this sheet. If you and other teachers have already discussed possible topics, you may want to list them yourself. Sheet 38–2 also asks students to answer questions about the audience and list new topics with the audience in mind.

4. Lead a class brainstorming session on possible topics by asking for suggestions from the class and writing all topics volunteered on the board. Stop after every five to critique them in terms of audience interest.

5. After ten minutes, narrow the list to three topics. Either let the class vote or select the topic yourself.

38–1. FLOW CHART FOR A CLASS PORTRAIT

THE OBJECTIVE: We will present a class portrait to an audience that consists of

_____ on _____ .

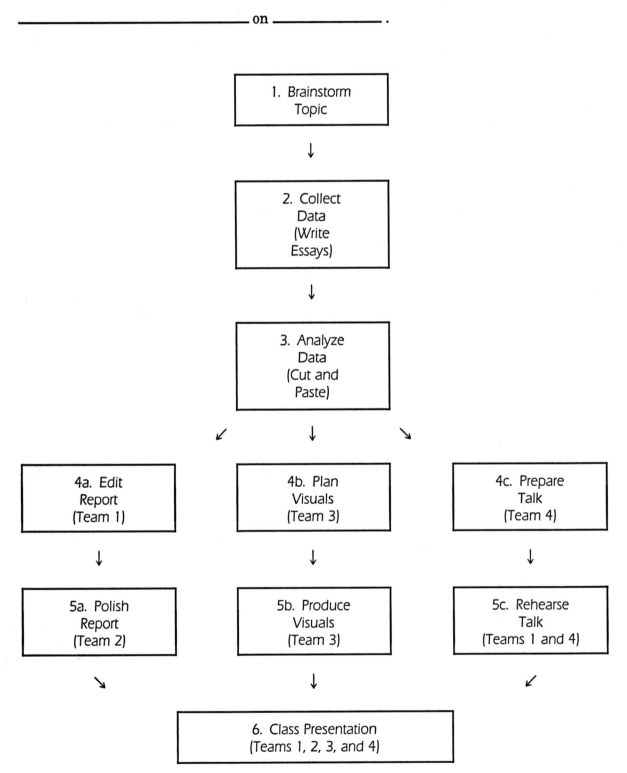

1. Brainstorm Topic

↓

2. Collect Data (Write Essays)

↓

3. Analyze Data (Cut and Paste)

↙ ↓ ↘

4a. Edit Report (Team 1)　　4b. Plan Visuals (Team 3)　　4c. Prepare Talk (Team 4)

↓　　↓　　↓

5a. Polish Report (Team 2)　　5b. Produce Visuals (Team 3)　　5c. Rehearse Talk (Teams 1 and 4)

↘　　↓　　↙

6. Class Presentation (Teams 1, 2, 3, and 4)

38−2. TOPIC AND AUDIENCE FOR A CLASS PORTRAIT

Directions: Your class is going to present a portrait of its opinions about a topic to a special audience. Answer the questions below to generate ideas for a class brainstorming session.

1. The audience is: _____

2. How many people are in it? (not counting teacher or students) _____

3. If the audience consists of more than one person, do the others come from a variety of backgrounds? If yes, what is common to all audience members?

   _____

   _____

   _____

4. List five issues relevant to the audience or of interest to them.

   a. _____

   b. _____

   c. _____

   d. _____

   e. _____

5. What two topics do you believe would *most* interest the audience? (You can use topics from the list above.)

   a. _____

   b. _____

6. Do you think everyone in the class can write an essay about these topics? Explain your answer and recommend a topic or topics accordingly.

   _____

   _____

   _____

7. Does each topic have at least two clearly opposing sides? If not, which might you want to eliminate?

   _____

Session 39. SNAPPING THE CLASS PORTRAIT

The organizational activities in the class project require data. Rather than spending time researching, students create the data themselves by writing individual essays that define their own positions on the chosen issue.

OBJECTIVES

The students will

- Define their personal stance on an issue
- Write a traditional essay explaining their opinion

SETTING THE STAGE

The class portrait presents the opinions of the class as a whole. The whole class, however, is comprised of individuals, each with distinctive ideas and ways to express thoughts. The final presentation will aim to portray this diversity concisely.

PROCEDURE

1. Tell the class they are now going to collect data for the class project by "snapping a portrait" of the class.
2. If you are collecting data from within your class, skip this step. If your class is capturing the opinions of another class,

    a. Brainstorm a list of questions each student will ask a member of the other class to elicit opinions on the issue. For consistency of data, the students must ask neither more nor fewer than these questions.

    b. List these questions on a sheet with space in between for notes, and photocopy or mimeograph enough copies for each student in your class.

    c. Hand out the questionnaires and remind your students to listen carefully to the interviewee, without reacting either verbally or nonverbally to what he or she says (to avoid influencing answers). Encourage students to capture as many accurate quotes as possible and to thank each interviewee for sharing his or her views.

    d. Bring the two classes together and divide students into pairs, with one student from each class in each pair.

    e. Give the class about ten minutes to conduct the interviews.

    f. Thank the other class for its cooperation; restore regular classes.

3. Write the following essay assignment on the board:

> Assume that you alone are writing to the audience. Write a traditional 300- to 400-word essay to express your own opinions on the established topic. (If you interviewed another student for this assignment, explain that student's opinions about the topic.) You will be graded on the merits of your individual work for this exercise.

4. Collect the essays and make enough copies for each student in class. Once the copies are made, evaluate the originals. The copies will be used in the next session.

Session 40. ORGANIZING THE DATA

In this session, students work in teams to categorize material for the class portrait. This is the third step in the presentation process.

OBJECTIVES

The students will

- Categorize information
- Organize information for conciseness

SETTING THE STAGE

In this session, you will hand out copies of all the essays to all your students and ask them to read through the stack. They will quickly discover that they have a lot of reading!

Remind the class that your audience has many responsibilities and simply cannot take the time to read through all the essays. To develop a clear, accurate, and accessible portrait for them, the class needs to make the information more concise. As a class, they will create a summary that is no more than fifteen pages long. How can this be done?

Categorize Information

Categories are one way to handle large amounts of information. To categorize, you look for similarities. The introductory paragraphs of the student essays, if they are well written, should provide an overview of the ideas in each paper and speed the process.

Identify the different opinions expressed and create categories accordingly. When you categorize, you lose detail, but you are better able to handle large amounts of data. The fewer the categories, the more detail you lose. The more numerous the categories, the more time and effort required to deal with the information.

Develop Statistics

Once categories are defined, you can develop statistics. The simplest statistic is a count of the number of people who hold a given opinion in a category. However, you can explore the data in a variety of ways.

Select Representative Pieces of Data

You can select direct quotes that represent the ideas and opinions of many others.

PROCEDURE

1. The day before the session, distribute copies of all the class essays to each student. Assign them to read all essays to become familiar with the material. Also, discuss categories using "Setting the Stage" as a guide. Ask students to begin thinking about categories as they read the essays. (If you have a very large class, you may want to split the essays into two groups so each student reads only half of them.)

2. On the day of the session, divide the class into teams of three or four members and give each team a copy of Sheet 40–1, "Creating Categories."

3. Let the teams brainstorm categories for about ten minutes, answering the questions on Sheet 40–1. Ask each team to send a member to the board to write its suggestions.

4. Review the suggestions with the class. Group common recommendations to shorten the list. Narrow the list, but leave at least five categories.

5. Ask for a new round of suggestions. Add them to the list. Review the entire list again, removing superfluous categories.

6. Assign each team to at least one category. Hand out Sheet 40–2, "One Piece of the Portrait." Tell students to cut and paste from the essays representative material for the category on the sheet (adding pages as necessary). Each team should provide three to five pages of materials. (Material may appear in more than one category.) Tell students you will not accept more than five pages from any team. If you have many teams, you will have fewer pages per category. The goal is to have a source document of fifteen to twenty pages, no more.

7. Collect the teams' work and evaluate each team's ability to create categories and select representative material. Then make four copies of this source material for the following session.

40–1. CREATING CATEGORIES

Directions: A category enables you to group similar material from many sources under a single heading. Answer the questions below to create categories for the class essays.

1. Look for common ideas in the material. These commonalities present possible categories. List at least five categories.

   _____

   _____

   _____

   _____

   _____

2. These categories may not include all material. List additional categories so all the material is represented.

   _____

   _____

3. Sometimes, in categorizing material, important ideas are distorted to fit the material into a category. Review the material and decide if your categories will force you to distort material. If so, you may want to create additional categories:

   _____

   _____

4. Write a short, descriptive heading for each category (using parallel construction). These will be written on the board for class discussion.

   _____   _____

   _____   _____

   _____   _____

   _____   _____

Names _____

_____   Date _____

40–2. ONE PIECE OF THE PORTRAIT

Your team's category: _____

Directions: Review the class essays and select material that relates to your team's category. Cut the material and paste it below. Next to each entry, write the initials of the author in case anyone should need to quote him or her. Use additional pages as needed.

Session 41. PRODUCING THE PORTRAIT

In this step of the presentation process, the class is divided into four teams. Objectives and procedures vary for each of the teams, so information is included under separate headings for subsessions 41A, 41B, 41C, and 41D.

SETTING THE STAGE

In an organization, every team is codependent. The decisions made in one team affect others. In this session, you divide your class into teams that perform different but related tasks. The success of the final presentation depends on how well these teams cooperate. Before beginning, you might want to review the whole presentation process on Sheet 38–1, "Flow Chart for a Class Portrait," to see how the teams are interrelated. This breakdown reflects how information is communicated in many organizations.

PROCEDURE

Review the presentation process with your class, and then divide the class into four teams:

- Team 1 edits the class portrait, making it accessible and concise.
- Team 2 creates statistics and polishes the final class portrait.
- Team 3 plans and prepares visual supports for the presentation.
- Team 4 prepares and delivers the oral presentation.

Approximately the same number of students should be in each group. You will need to follow separate procedures outlined in the next four subsessions.

Session 41A. THE FIRST EDITING TEAM

The first editing team is responsible for consolidating information in the class summary produced in Session 40 into a concise, accessible document.

OBJECTIVES

The students will

- Organize material for presentation.
- Edit material to make it more concise and focused.

SETTING THE STAGE

The final presentation is structured by its *framework*, which this team will create. If this framework is illogical or incomplete, the efforts of all other teams—no matter how excellent—will be wasted. That is why it is critical to pay attention to the beginning.

PROCEDURE

1. Give the team copies of the class portrait summary, one for each member. Also hand out Sheet 41A–1, "Creating a Framework," and tell the team to use it to help organize the material. The result should be the headline (title) and a list of presentation headings, which the team should check with you for approval.
2. Once you approve the organizational framework, the team should report its results to the other teams so everyone is functioning within the same framework.
3. Hand out Sheet 41A–2, "Editing a Category," to each member of the editing group, to guide individuals as they edit their assigned category or categories.
4. Once all categories have been edited, the team should assemble the material within the framework it set up and pass it along to the second editing team.
5. For the next step, the first editing team serves as a practice audience for the oral presentation team, offering suggestions for improving the presentation.

Names _____

_____ Date _____

41A–1. CREATING A FRAMEWORK

Directions: Your team's job is to turn the categorized raw data into a written report that you will give to the audience. Review your objective. Then, as a group, choose answers to the questions below to define the structure of your class portrait report.

1. What is the best order for presenting your categories?

   _____ alphabetically

   _____ by time sequence

   _____ by order of importance

   _____ other: _____

2. List the categories below in presentation order. Note that the introduction is already listed. It will be written last, by another team.

   a. ___Introduction_____

   b. _____

   c. _____

   d. _____

   e. _____

   f. _____

   g. _____

   h. _____

   i. _____

   j. _____

3. Are the headings parallel in construction? If not, rewrite them in the blanks in question 5, making sure they are consistent.

4. Each member of your group will take at least one category and compress the material so the final portrait is *no more than ten pages long*. Before you can begin, however, you must decide the following:

   a. What format will the final portrait use?

      _____ essay _____ bulleted summary _____ mixed format

   b. Will there be subheadings? _____ Yes _____ No

   c. What point of view will material be presented from?

   _____ "we" _____ "the class" _____ "I" _____ "they" (another class)

5. Consider the size of each category (see question 2). Decide how many pages you want the category reduced to and write that below. Remember, the entire report after your team edits it should be no more than ten pages long, excluding the introduction, which the second editing team writes.

Category: **Number of pages:**

   a. ____Introduction_____   _____

   b. _____   _____

   c. _____   _____

   d. _____   _____

   e. _____   _____

   f. _____   _____

   g. _____   _____

   h. _____   _____

   i. _____   _____

   j. _____   _____

6. What title do you want to use for the presentation? This will serve as the title of both the oral presentation and the written report. In your group, brainstorm possible titles and write the best three below:

   a. _____

   b. _____

   c. _____

7. Choose your favorite title and check it (along with your presentation headings above) with your teacher before telling it to the other teams.

   Our favorite title: _____

   _____

41A–2. EDITING A CATEGORY

Directions: Cut and paste material from the class summary for the category (or categories) assigned to you. Reduce it to the size agreed on by your group. Add any subheadings and text you feel necessary to achieve your presentation objective (keeping in mind decisions your team has made about the format of the report.) Use quotes when possible to represent opinions. When you are done, write a *short* overview for the category.

Overview: _____

_____

_____

_____

Selected and Edited Material: (Continue on additional pages as necessary.)

_____

_____

_____

_____

_____

_____

_____

_____

_____

_____

_____

_____

_____

Session 41B. THE SECOND EDITING TEAM

The second editing team computes statistics while waiting for the first editing team to provide the report. It then polishes the report and writes an introduction to it.

OBJECTIVES

The students will

- Create statistics and word pictures from raw data
- Write an overview
- Edit material for final presentation

SETTING THE STAGE

Statistics make large amounts of data accessible. This team will create statistics to help in the presentation before polishing the report that comes from the first editing team.

PROCEDURE

1. Give this team the same copies of the class summary you gave to the first team. Also hand out Sheet 41B–1, "Statistically Speaking." This team can use the sheet and the raw data to begin creating statistics before they learn the presentation categories from the first editing team. However, this team cannot complete its work without the categories from the first editing team.

2. Once the team has finished Sheet 41B–1, check its work before it discusses its results with the other teams.

3. Hand out Sheet 41B–2, "Checklist for a Final Written Report," which explains the steps this team should take to create the final product. (If you have word processing equipment available at any stage of their work, it should prove helpful.) Suggest that the team first work on drafts (cutting and pasting material) before creating a final product. They must see that it contains statistics and illustrations (which can be graphs, tables, etc.).

4. This group also needs to draft an introduction (using Sheet 41B–2) after discussing material with the oral presentation group to make sure both groups are taking a similar approach.

5. Work with the team to perfect grammar and spelling. If possible, get a neatly typed final copy (word processing makes this easier) and have the group proofread this final copy, making any necessary corrections.

6. Make copies of the final written report for the class and your special guest(s).

Names _____

_____ Date _____

41B–1. STATISTICALLY SPEAKING

Directions: Your first assignment is to help the audience quickly grasp the portrait by creating statistics for them. When you have completed the sheet, check your work with your teacher. Then give copies of the completed sheet to the visuals team and the oral presentation team so they can use your work in their parts of the presentation.

1. Look through the individual essays. Did anyone use statistics? If they did, record the ones you think will be useful in the presentation:

   a. _____

   b. _____

   c. _____

   d. _____

   e. _____

2. Can you create any word pictures for these statistics? If so, write them below:

   _____

   _____

   _____

   _____

   _____

   _____

3. Quantity statistics:

   a. Total number of pages of individual essays: _____

   b. Estimated number of pages in final written report: _____

   c. Subtract to find the difference: _____

   d. Divide item c by item a and multiply by 100 for percentage reduced: _____

   e. Fill in: "We started with _____ pages of work, which we edited down to _____ pages, a _____ % reduction in the pages you need to read."

4. The first editing group will tell you the categories they are using to group material. How many individual essays support each category? (Note that a single essay can support more than one category.)

Category: **Number in Support:**

a. _____   _____

b. _____   _____

c. _____   _____

d. _____   _____

e. _____   _____

f. _____   _____

g. _____   _____

h. _____   _____

i. _____   _____

Total number of essays that support something: _____

5. Compute the percent of the class supporting each category. To make the calculation, divide the number of essays supporting each category by the total number of essays that support something and multiply by 100.

Category: **Percent of Class Support:**

a. _____   _____

b. _____   _____

c. _____   _____

d. _____   _____

e. _____   _____

f. _____   _____

g. _____   _____

h. _____   _____

i. _____   _____

6. Discuss your statistics with the visual and oral presentation groups and provide them with a copy of these sheets (after your teacher checks and approves your figures).

Name _____ Date _____

41B–2. CHECKLIST FOR A FINAL WRITTEN REPORT

_____ 1. Review the revised material provided to you by the first editing team. Edit it to make it more concise and clearer, if possible. Your work at this time is still drafting (not polishing), so use cutting and pasting techniques to save time and effort.

_____ 2. Add any statistics and word pictures that you created, as appropriate.

_____ 3. The visuals team should have already given you suggestions for illustrations and figures. Incorporate these as appropriate, indicating them (if they are not available yet) with the estimated amount of white space necessary and a notation in brackets, as in the following example:

[Visual: graph showing % of class supporting categories]

_____ 4. Draft an introduction to the report, incorporating the statistics you generated about class support in each category and the page reduction the class achieved, as computed on Sheet 41B–1, item 3e. Make sure that the introduction makes clear the purpose of the report. Discuss the introduction with the oral presentation team to ensure that the two teams are following the same framework.

_____ 5. Prepare a final draft of the introduction.

_____ 6. Check spelling and grammar and do any other polishing necessary to create a final draft of the report.

_____ 7. Type or very neatly write the final draft (see if you can use a word processing program or have it typed by someone who can).

_____ 8. Proofread the final copy for spelling errors and typos and correct them neatly. (Or correct the errors on disk and print the report again.) Make enough copies for each member of the audience, the class, and your teacher.

_____ 9. Bind the reports in folders or staple on cover pages.

Session 41C. THE VISUALS TEAM

The third team creates visuals to support the presentation. They design and provide both transparencies for the oral presentations and illustrations for the printed report. If transparencies are difficult to produce, flipcharts or posters make effective substitutes.

OBJECTIVE

The students will create visuals to support a presentation.

SETTING THE STAGE

In a professional presentation, visuals are often used to support both the written and spoken material. Usually, identical visuals are used to reinforce important points in both versions.

PROCEDURE

1. Give each member of the team a copy of the class summary (created in Session 40) and Sheet 41C–1, "Planning Visuals for a Presentation." At this time you should also provide team members with multiple copies of Sheet 41C–2, "Visuals Planning Page." Team members should begin by reviewing the unedited summary and the objective. They can then begin to plan and gather material as guided by the worksheet. If your computer lab is equipped to scan visuals onto disk for manipulation, try to arrange time (and training, if necessary) for this team to work in the lab.

2. As soon as the first editing team has its title and categories ready, they should meet with the visuals team to give them the information and answer any questions the visuals team may have. Similarly, they should meet with the second editing team when they have their initial statistics prepared.

3. The visuals team is responsible for suggesting transparencies (or some other appropriate media) to the oral presentation team. These teams should meet to discuss these and decide which ones to produce.

4. The visuals team is also responsible for suggesting illustrations (figures) to the second editing team for their final written report. When they have their suggestions ready, have them meet with the second editing team to discuss and decide which illustrations to produce.

5. Once the list of transparencies and illustrations to be produced is definite, hand out Sheet 41C–3, "Checklist for Producing Visuals." Team members may either produce the materials themselves (using pen and ink, a computer, copying machines, etc.) or supervise production by an art class or some other group. Team members with fewer artistic skills should concentrate on proofreading the materials.

6. As soon as possible, the visuals team should give their visuals to the oral presentation team so they can rehearse with them and to the second editing team so they can prepare their final report. If students are left without anything to do, they can join the audience for the oral presentation team or help the second editing team with final production of the written report (including any collating, stapling, etc.).

Names _____

_____ Date _____

41C–1. PLANNING VISUALS FOR A PRESENTATION

Directions: Follow the instructions below to plan visuals for both the written report and oral presentation. Make sure your suggestions can be produced within the school.

1. Review the objective and the class summary materials. Brainstorm a list of specific materials you can use as sources for visuals. For example, you might list specific magazine or newspaper headlines, photos you know, or likely sources of what you want.

   a. _____

   b. _____

   c. _____

   d. _____

   e. _____

   f. _____

   g. _____

2. As a team, collect these materials (and any others you may come across that would fit). Make copies of them for cutting and pasting. (Or scan them onto a disk if you have access to that technology.)

3. Can you use any of this material to illustrate the title? If so, what? If not, how else might you be able to illustrate it?

   _____

   _____

4. The first editing team will provide you a list of presentation categories and, later, material for each one. You can feature major and minor headings on a transparency. Sketch possible transparencies on Sheet 41C–2, "Visual Planning Page," using additional copies of it as necessary. Sketch in or note any appropriate art to illustrate the text.

5. The second editing team will provide you with statistics. Discuss them with the team and decide how best to portray them. Sketch graphs (for instance, pie charts for the percentages) on the "Visual Planning Page." Remember that you can often illustrate statistics with appropriate graphics.

41C–1. Planning Visuals for a Presentation Continued

6. As a team, review your suggested visuals for both groups and decide which visuals you want to recommend to the oral presentation team and the second editing team. (For important points, you may want to recommend identical visuals.) When you meet with them, show them the sketches of your recommended visuals (using as many copies as necessary of the "Visual Planning Page"). Put a large X over any transparencies you agree to eliminate. Sketch in any new ones you decide to add. Then give these teams copies of the planned visuals for their presentation.

7. Your illustrations for the written report need to have captions or titles. You will also need to check that appropriate figure references have been provided in the text (for example, See Figure 1: [Title of Figure]). Figures may be drawings, graphs, tables, and so on. Below, list titles or captions for the figures you plan. Use parallel construction.

Figure 1. _____

Figure 2. _____

Figure 3. _____

Figure 4. _____

Figure 5. _____

Figure 6. _____

Give a copy of this list to the second editing team.

41C–2. VISUAL PLANNING PAGE

Visual #

Visual #

Visual #

Visual #

Visual #

Visual #

41C–3. CHECKLIST FOR PRODUCING VISUALS

_____ 1. If you are working with another class (for instance, an art class), concentrate on creating the transparencies (or posters) first. Have each member of the team discuss one or two transparencies with a person who will produce them. Try to explain exactly what was envisioned, providing a rough sketch and, if possible, copies of material for cutting and pasting. Tell the people producing the transparencies exactly how long they have to finish them.

_____ 2. If your team is producing the material, decide on formats and begin work.

_____ 3. Carefully proofread all visuals for mistakes. You do not want a mistake projected in large letters for everyone to see. Make any corrections necessary and proofread the material again. Use more than one proofreader on every piece.

_____ 4. Give the completed transparencies to the oral presentation team (they need time to rehearse with them).

_____ 5. If you have access to a copying machine that reduces, use it to make reduced copies of the transparencies that are also going to be used as figures in the written report. You may want to create black line boxes around the figures. Try to keep the same size box throughout when possible. Quality black line boxes can be created

   • On the typewriter (put paper in vertically and then horizontally)

   • Using a graphics software program

   • With a ruler and T-square (and black ink or press-on black rule)

   • By photocopying a box from a magazine or other source

_____ 6. If necessary, make changes to the visuals, using cutting and pasting techniques rather than redoing work.

_____ 7. Give the illustrations to the second editing team. You should already have given them a list of titles or captions for the figures.

_____ 8. Once the figures have been added to the text, check to make sure the figure title matches the correct figure.

Session 41D. THE ORAL PRESENTATION TEAM

The fourth team plans, rehearses, and (in the following session) actually presents the class portrait to the guest audience, incorporating the work of all the teams.

OBJECTIVES

The students will

- Plan and rehearse an oral presentation
- Use visual and written supports

SETTING THE STAGE

The most stimulating visuals and exciting topics in the world will not keep an audience engaged for long unless the presentation itself is interesting. Making a presentation compelling is a challenge for most students.

For this session, students may *not* use any techniques from the world of entertainment—they may not sing, dance, or perform dramatic scenes. They must rely on basic communication skills they have learned to make presentations interesting.

PROCEDURE

1. Give each member of the team a copy of the class summary produced in Session 40, as well as Sheet 41D–1, "Presenting the Class Portrait." It will lead the team through the planning and rehearsal stages.

2. As soon as the first editing team has prepared its categories, have it meet with the oral presentation team to provide this information and answer any questions. Similarly, as soon as the second editing team has prepared its statistics, have it meet with the oral presentation team to give them the information.

3. As soon as the visuals team has ready its recommendations for visuals to support the presentation, have it meet with the oral presentation team to discuss the recommendations and decide together which visuals to produce.

4. When the oral presentation team begins to practice, you may want to sit in occasionally, helping to time the presentation. Feel free to suggest how to make the presentation more interesting, and encourage the first editing team to assume this role (in a positive way) when they become the audience.

216

Names _____

Date _____

41D–1. PRESENTING THE CLASS PORTRAIT

Directions: You will be making a fifteen- to twenty-minute presentation of the class portrait to the guest(s). As a team, read through the points below and follow the steps to plan your presentation.

1. Making a team presentation is different from making an individual presentation. All speakers must work together. Each one should build on what was said before, and no one should unnecessarily repeat what was said before.

2. Read the first version of the class portrait carefully. The first editing team is selecting information from it for a more concise report. You may be asked about material that is not in the final written report, however, so you need to know the material well. You may also decide to present slightly different material.

3. Review the objective of your presentation as a team. Note that you are representing the class's portrait, not your own. You may personally disagree with certain positions, but to maintain the integrity of the portrait you need to present all points of view objectively that make up the class portrait. Continually remind each other to be fair and accurate in presenting material.

4. The first editing team will present you with a title and an organizational framework for how it intends to write the report. Discuss the framework with them and try to follow it. Although your material will not be identical to their report, it should be consistent with it, since the audience will be seeing both.

5. Using the following framework as a guide, list how your team will present the portrait. Create as many presentation categories as you need. Note that the introduction, overview, and conclusion have already been added. You will fill in the speakers later.

Title: _____

Category: **Speaker:**

a. ___Introduction_____ _____

b. ___Overview_____ _____

c. _____ _____

d. _____ _____

e. _____ _____

f. _____ _____

g. _____ _____

h. _____ _____

i. _____ _____

j. ___Conclusion_____ _____

6. Now assign each member of the team at least one category to present, according to these guidelines:

   • The person assigned the introduction will also present the conclusion.

   • Any other person assigned more than one category must be assigned consecutive categories (for instance, 3 and 4 or 6 and 7). This is to reduce confusion from speakers bouncing up and down.

7. Write the speakers' names next to their categories. Each person should now outline his or her assigned categories.

TIP: In your individual presentations, always try to provide a framework or context immediately. Use overviews that combine material. Use details and quotes to support points, but add perspective to those points.

SPECIAL TIPS FOR THE PERSON DOING THE INTRODUCTION/CONCLUSION:

Your teacher will greet the guest(s) and introduce you. You should begin by briefly introducing the controversial issue—but quickly suggest standing back to review how the portrait came to be.

Describe how many teams worked together and what they did (without identifying specific people). You may want to use a transparency or poster that illustrates the overall presentation process.

The second editing team will be giving your team a statistic that shows how much you reduced the original data. Use the statistic and explain why it is important to be concise for your guest(s).

Inform your guest(s) that the students presenting are doing so on behalf of the class as a whole. You should then introduce each speaker in the speaking order and briefly describe what he or she will discuss.

When all the speakers are finished, you may want to summarize the issue briefly. Acknowledge everyone's contributions to the class effort. Tell the guest(s) they will receive written summaries of the presentation. Thank everyone for their time and attention. This conclusion should be very brief—no more than ninety seconds.

---

8. Cut and paste your individual outlines together on separate sheets of paper to create a team outline.

9. Review the team's outline and decide how much time to devote to each category. Next to each category, write the number of minutes you want to allot to it. (Use pencil.) Try to use whole minutes, but, if necessary, you may use half minutes—no smaller, however. Remember that the entire presentation, including introduction and conclusion, can take no longer than twenty minutes.

10. Some categories may have too much material to present in the allotted time. As a team, discuss how to resolve this. Adjust allocations if necessary.

41D–1. Presenting the Class Portrait Continued

11. The visuals team will suggest visuals (transparencies or posters) to support your presentation. In your meeting with them, suggest variations or request additional visuals, if necessary. Once you and the visuals team are agreed on what visuals to use, list them on your presentation outline.

12. Prepare your individual presentations. Rehearse your presentation alone several times, trying to keep under the allocated time. If you wish, ask a classmate to time your presentation.

13. Practice the presentation as a team. Each speaker should stand up in turn. Note the time each speaker begins and ends, and write how much time he or she actually took. At this point, do not cut anyone off or interrupt.

14. Review how long each speaker took, making suggestions on how to shorten or lengthen the talk. Also offer suggestions on how to make each part more interesting. Remember, you must engage and hold your audience's attention.

15. As a team, run through the presentation. Again note the time taken for each topic, and this time pay careful attention to how each speaker looks (gestures, body language) and sounds (monotone, too fast, too slow, too many "ums" or "you knows"). Give each speaker feedback once the entire presentation is over.

16. Do the presentation with the first editing team for your audience. When the whole presentation is complete, ask the editing team members to criticize your presentation for logic, pacing, and visual appeal. Again check your timing. Is the presentation under twenty minutes? Is it interesting?

17. When the visuals team gives you the visuals, try out the presentation before the entire class. (Ask someone from the visuals team to switch transparencies or hold up posters.) Get feedback from the class. Again, is the presentation under twenty minutes?

18. If your teacher advises, practice the presentation one more time.

YOU'RE NOW READY TO REPRESENT YOUR CLASS!

Session 42. PRESENTING THE PORTRAIT, AND REVIEW

The class portrait is complete and ready for presentation! Once the presentation is over, you should review the process with the class and discuss improvements to review the communication skills your students have developed.

OBJECTIVES

The students will

- Evaluate the effectiveness of a presentation
- Analyze the process of working as part of a team

SETTING THE STAGE

Students applied almost all of the skills they learned in the sessions of this book in developing and presenting their class portrait.

- In their small teams, they used the skills of listening and speaking.
- In deciding on a topic and developing it, they used brainstorming techniques, analyzed alternatives, and made group decisions.
- In developing and producing visuals, they used their visual skills.
- All groups, but especially the editing teams, used cutting and pasting skills. They also used visual elements in text, like bullets, headings, and white space.
- All worked within limits to present information concisely.
- Your speakers presented information, paying attention to body language and other presentation skills.
- The class as a whole analyzed an audience, set an objective, and evaluated whether they met it.

You have taken your class a long way. Congratulations!

PROCEDURE

1. Before the day of the presentation, make copies of the written report for everyone, including your guest(s). Arrange for an overhead projector for the transparencies. Urge the class to be supportive of the

presenting team; remind students that the team is representing them. Finally, remind the guest(s) of the appointment.

2. On the day of the presentation, greet the guest(s). Explain how long the presentation will take, and then turn the presentation over to the student responsible for the introduction. Write down the beginning time.

3. When the presentation is complete, write down the time, and ask your guest(s) if they have any questions for the speakers.

4. When all questions have been answered, thank your guests for their time and attention. Give them copies of the written report and ask them to review it in their spare time, but request that they get back to you with their comments. (Share comments with the class when you receive them.)

5. Hand out Sheet 42–1, "How Could We Make It Better?," and use it as a starting point to review the presentation. Tell the presenters whether they stayed within the time guidelines. If not, what was the effect on the audience? Praise special efforts, particularly by people not seen during the presentation.

6. Review the communication skills developed in the unit, using "Setting the Stage" as your guide.

Name _____ Date _____

42–1. HOW COULD WE MAKE IT BETTER?

Directions: Usually, presentations do not simply end. The organization reviews what it did and looks for ways to improve the process. Your thoughts will help next year's class give a better presentation—and help you to understand better communication.

1. Did the class achieve the presentation objective? Justify your answer.

   _____

   _____

   _____

2. On a scale of 1 to 5, how good was the presentation?

   Excellent   1   2   3   4   5   Poor

3. On a scale of 1 to 5, how important was your team's contribution?

   Very important   1   2   3   4   5   Unimportant

4. What was the most important lesson you learned about working as part of a team effort on this presentation?

   _____

   _____

5. Which team did you work on? _____

6. Describe the strengths of your team and its work: _____

   _____

   _____

7. How could your team improve? _____

   _____

   _____

8. If your class were to repeat this process for another topic, what would you suggest it do differently to make the presentation even more effective? Try to make three suggestions.

   a. _____

   b. _____

   c. _____